Beautiful Mosaic Flowers

A step-by step guide

Sigalit Eshet

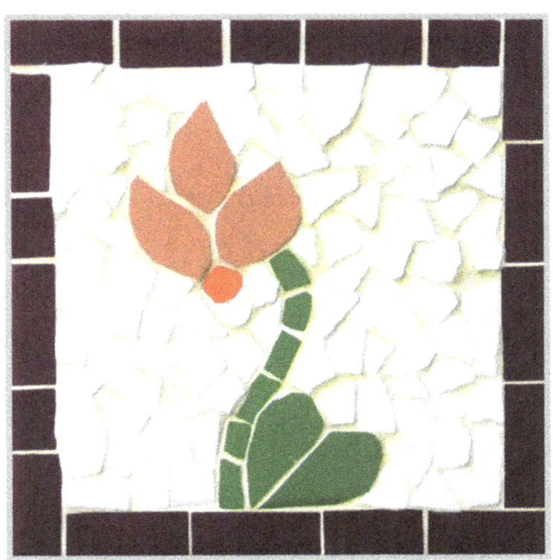

First Digital Edition: 2012

First Print Edition: 2014

Disclaimer

All do-it-yourself activities involve risk, and your safety is your own responsibility, including proper use of equipment and safety gear, and determining whether you have adequate skill and experience.

Some of the resources used for these projects are dangerous unless used properly and with adequate pre-cautions, including safety gear.

Some illustrative photos do not depict safety precautions or equipment, in order to show the project step more clearly.

Some projects are user-submitted, and appearance of a project in this format does not indicate it has been checked for safety or functionality. Use of the instructions and suggestions is at your own risk.

I disclaim all responsibility for any resulting damage, injury, or expense. It is your responsibility to make sure that your activities comply with all applicable laws.

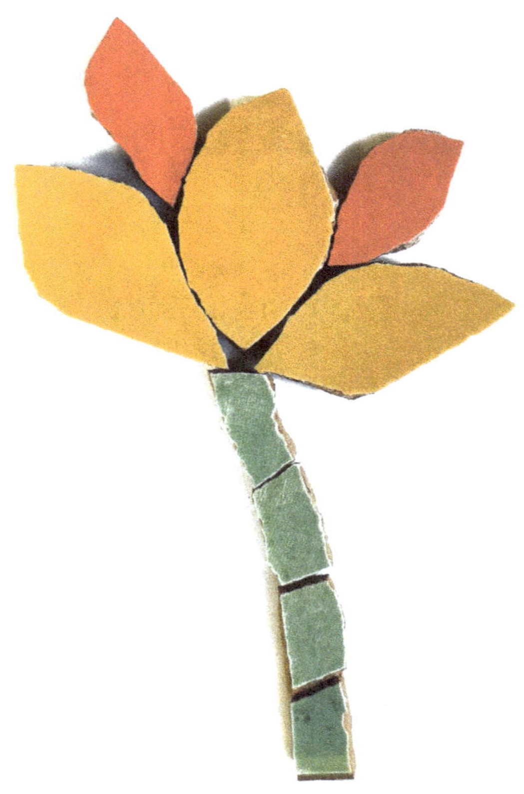

Content:

Introduction: 5

Mosaic tools and equipment   6

What base should I use?   11

Materials   12

How do I start?   13

Using the mosaic cutter   14

Cutting petals: Cone petals   15

Cutting petals: Sharp petal shape   18

Cutting petals: Rounded petals   22

Cutting petals: Drop-shaped petals   25

Cutting petals: Rose   27

Project sample   30

Mosaic flower works   33

Summary   43

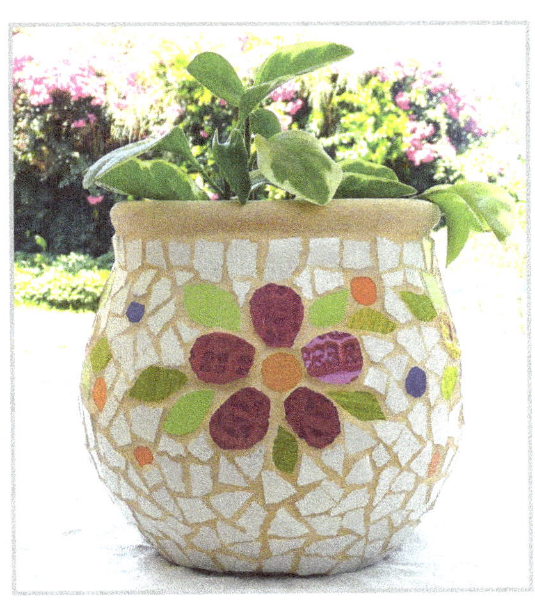

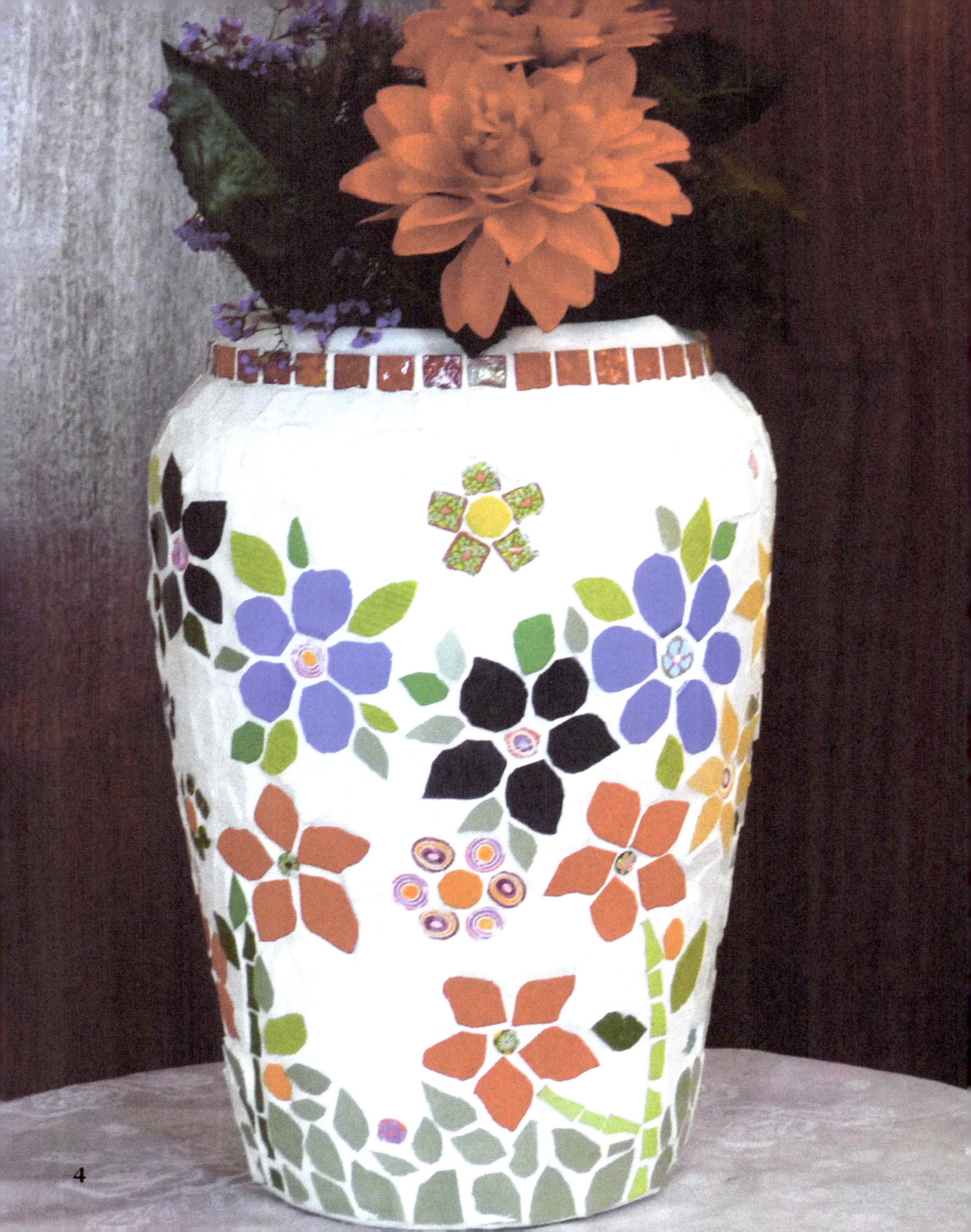

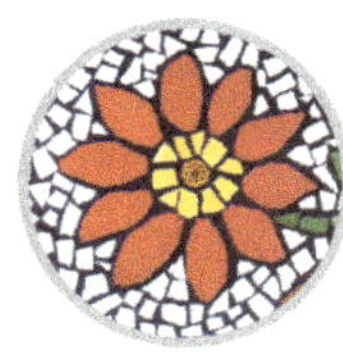

Introduction:

"Mosaic making with love": I believe in, teach, and work according to this expression. I'm glad to have you with me on my journey to create beautiful art with these colorful stones. I sincerely hope you enjoy the book, and that it helps you take a step toward creating a great mosaic work of art.

If you think cutting mosaic flowers sounds too difficult, then this book is for you! This practical, easy-to-follow guide will take you through the process of making lovely mosaic flowers from start to finish.

In this book, you will find cutting techniques along with helpful diagrams, photos, and instructions. As you practice, you will see that the tile cutting becomes faster, and you will eventually create beautiful flower petals with ease! The rest of the creation is up to you—you can create pots, plates, murals, lamps, and countless other gorgeous decorations once you have nailed the basics of mosaic tile cutting. I guarantee that you will get a lot of compliments as you create your own mosaic flower garden! Don't buy expensive art works – do it yourself!

My name is Sigalit; I'm a mosaic artist, and have taught mosaics for several years.

This book was born out of my desire to give my students a simple way to cut flowers, which they love so much. I saw their fear of trying to cut flowers, thinking that the work involved in cutting the small, intricate pieces would be too complicated, worried that they would not succeed.

I have developed techniques that anyone who know how to use a mosaic cutter can implement in order to make colorful mosaic flowers.

Hope I have intrigued you! I recommend trying to cut the flowers in the books for more practice—start with the sharp petal shape, and once you become more comfortable, try the rose.

Let's get to work!

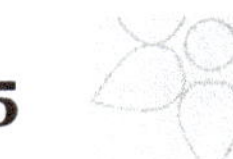

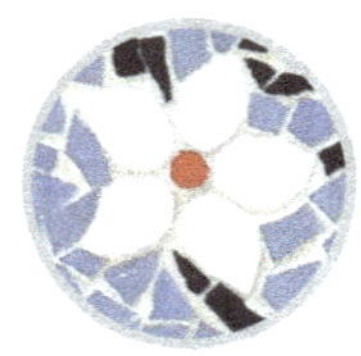

Mosaic tools and equipment

Basic mosaic tools are inexpensive and easily attainable (In the list below I added some materials for advanced use also):

Cutting tools:

Mosaic tile cutter – for cutting and grinding ceramic tiles. You can get these in hardware stores.

Wheeled glass nipper – for cutting glass and plates.

Ceramic cutting machine – for advanced cutters, used to cut ceramic into straight and accurate tiles.

Hammer – for cutting thick ceramic, or when you want to cut random shapes. Please note that when you cut ceramic with a hammer, you should wrap the ceramic with an old towel and place it on top of a thick wood or metal surface.

Safety equipment:

Safety Goggles – to protect your eyes from ceramic fragments. Use it when you cut the ceramic.

Dust mask – used this when making the grout.

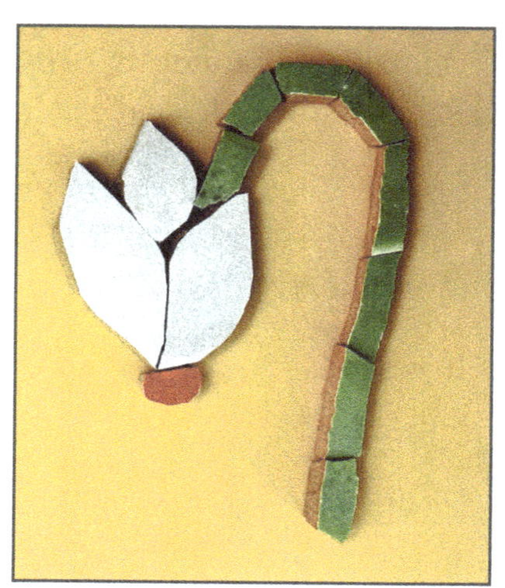

Preparation tools

Pencil – for drawing the desired pattern on the substrate material.

Ruler – to mark straight lines.

Latex gloves – to protect your hands from scratches and dirt.

Rubber gloves – put these on before you start working with grout.

Carbon paper – to copy your design from paper onto your substrate material.

Plastic tools – for grout mixing, tile collecting and gluing.

Small brush – for cleaning the surface from dust and small particles.

Thin screwdriver – for cleaning tile adhesive residue.

Tweezers – for the placement of small parts.

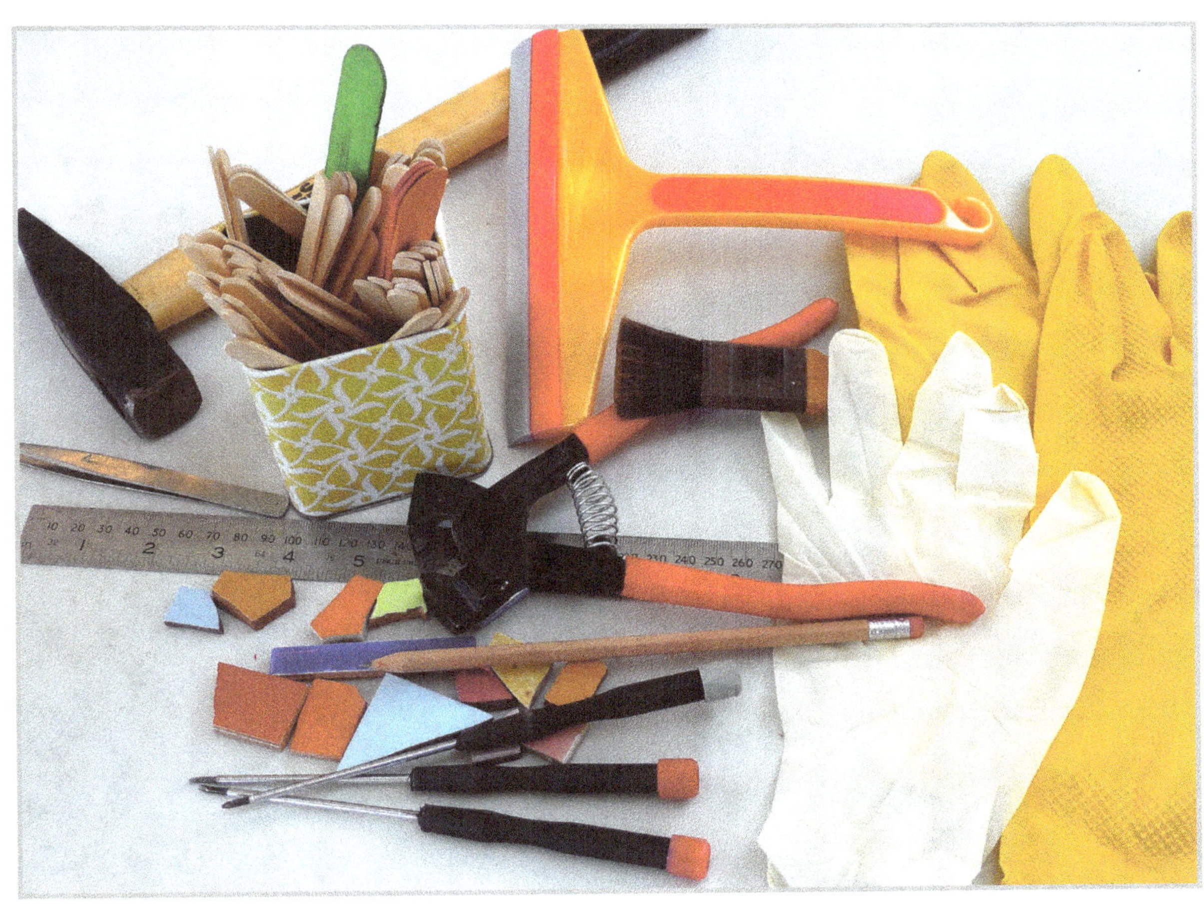

Adhesives

For proper use of glue, always read the manufacturer's instructions. Use the glue that is most comfortable for you to work. It is very important to adjust the glue to the platform on which you are working. On wooden bases we use white glue—for indoor works only that will be away from water and direct sunlight. When we make a metal base mosaic we will use adhesive tile—this way the table can stand outside in all weather conditions with no problem.

PVA glue – for sticking ceramic tiles onto a wood surface.

Paintbrush – for adhesive application.

Mosaic tile adhesive – for sticking ceramic tiles onto metal, clay or ceramic pots

Glass glue – for sticking tiles onto a glass substrate (like E6000).

Wooden mixing sticks – for mixing grout and applying the tile adhesive.

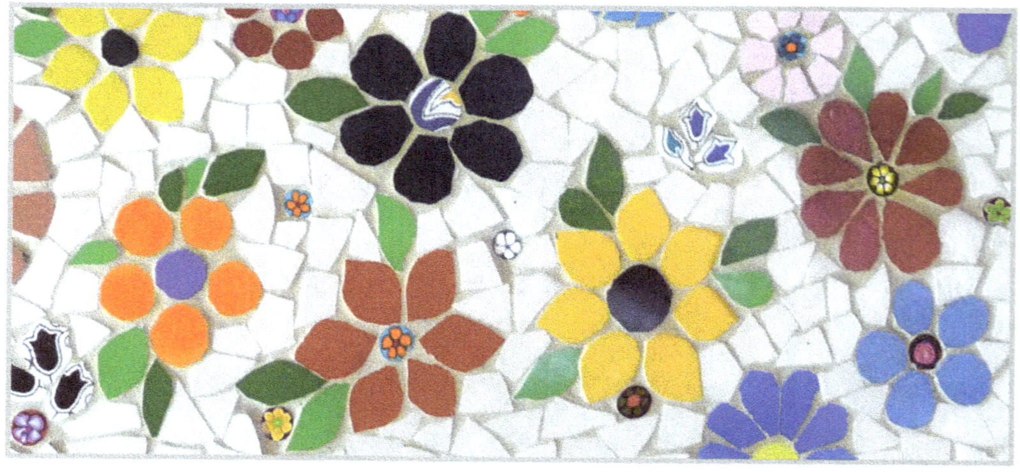

Grout

Grout – to fill the gaps between the tiles.

NOTE: There are different types of grout. Most of them come in powdered form, which you will need to mix with water according the manufacturer's instructions. Grout also comes in different colors, so choose the right color for your work. You can also mix acrylic paint into white grout to make your own custom colored grout, but if you do this, be sure that the final work is not exposed to the sun or water.

Working with the grout can be messy, so wear appropriate clothing and put on gloves before starting.

Water – for making grout and cleaning.

Small squeegee – for gripping and putting the grout on straight surfaces.

Sponge or cotton rags – for grout cleaning.

Old newspapers – to put under your work to maintain a clean work surface.

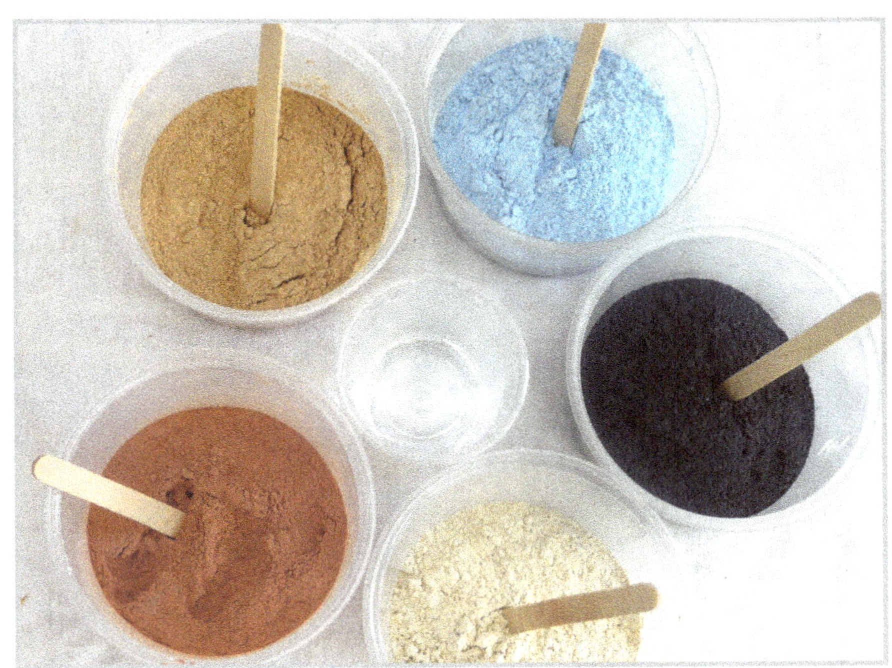

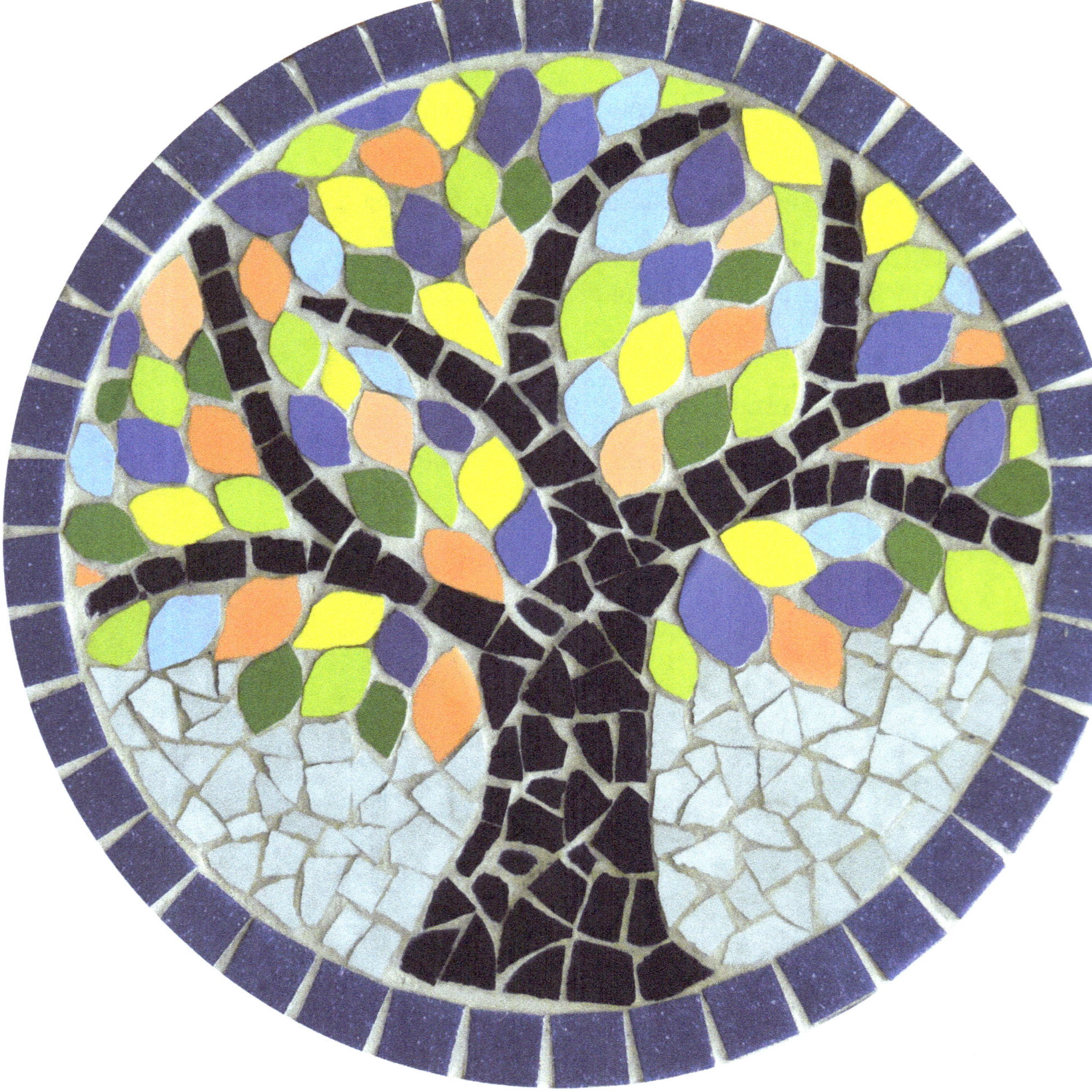

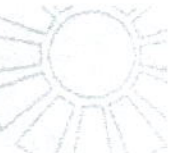

What base should I use?

Mosaic tiles can stick to almost any surface. I prefer to separate bases into two categories: straight and curved.

Beginners should start with a straight surface: board, plywood or an MDF base to create things like picture frames, small mirror frame or bases for hot pots. Once you grasp these basics, you can do a mosaic table or other furniture like a chest of drawers, or chairs. Be mindful that wood-based mosaic projects should be displayed indoors only.

A curved surface could be something like a terracotta pot, or any bowl or vessel made out of clay, ceramic or glass. The working technique is the same. We can put our pot on a rotating base such as a pottery wheel in order to make our work easier.

There is another kind of mosaic: on a tapestry mesh. This is the basis for works like wall tiles, stairs or large wall murals. We stick the mosaic on a mesh cut to the shape and size of the desired surface, and after it dries it is glued into place with mosaic tile adhesive.

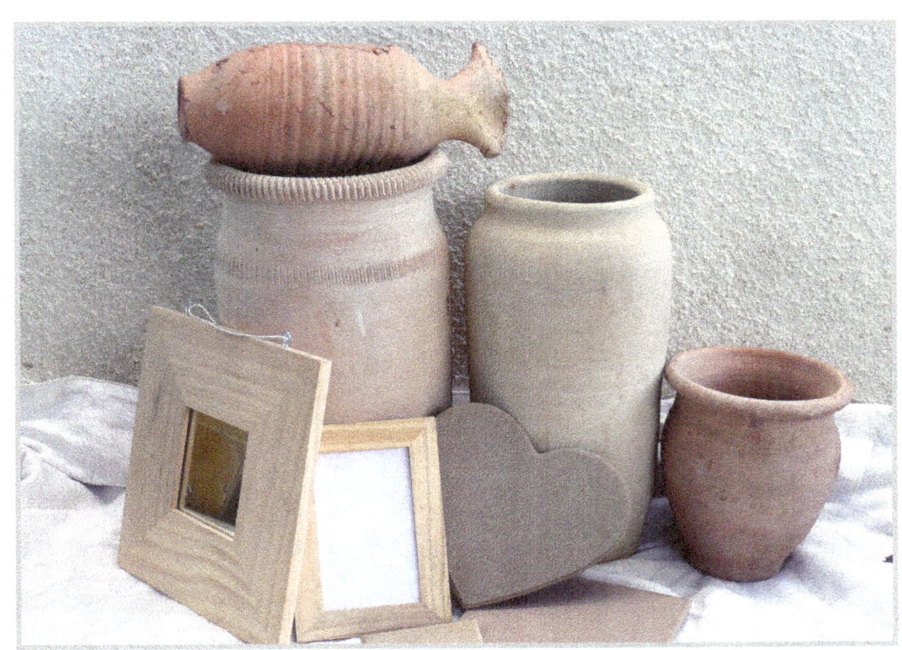

Materials

Mosaic materials are varied and include:

Colorful ceramic tiles – in different shapes and sizes.

Glass tiles – these come in uniform size squares and in many colors. They have one smooth flat side (which should face up), and a rough side (faces down; this is the side to which glue is applied).

Stained glass – comes in many colors and textures.

Ceramic square tiles – available in many colors, textures and shapes; come mostly on a square mesh.

Ceramic or porcelain plates – using safety precautions, these can be broken or used to cut your own tiles from.

Broken cups – for more abstract, non-uniform pieces in your mosaic, you may wish to break your own glass.

Beads, seashells, glass beads, buttons, glass nuggets –use this to decorate and enrich your work.

Mirrors – breaking mirrors might be considered bad luck, but they add a beautiful reflective touch to any mosaic piece.

Polymer clay – use polymer clay like Fimo to create your own designs, or decorate your mosaic work.

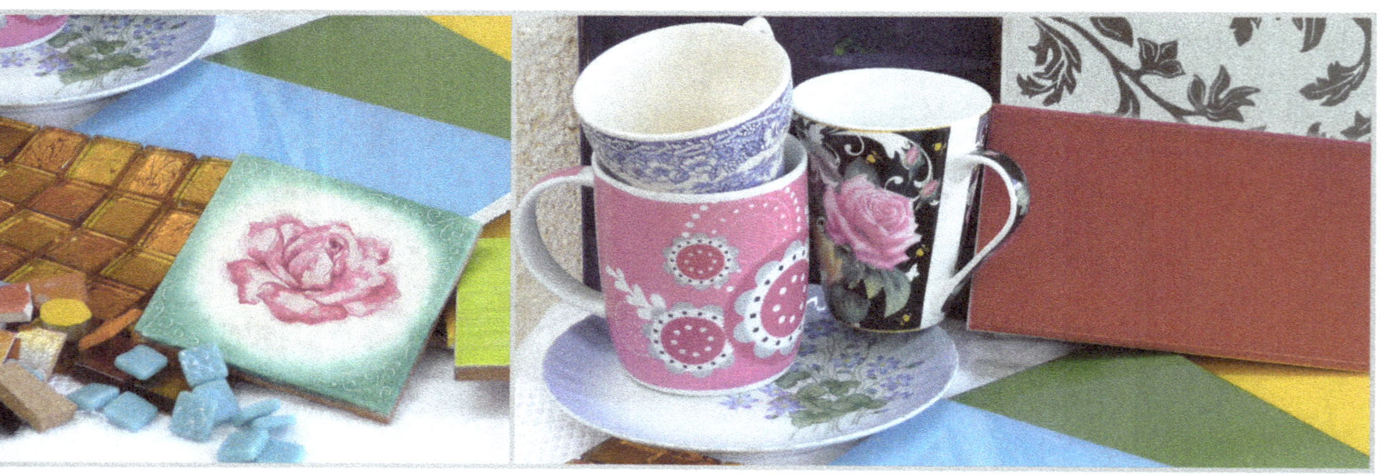

How do I start?

After getting to know the working materials, we can begin selecting the working surface. I suggest choosing a flat wooden platform for your first mosaic piece.

In this book we will learn how to cut ceramic flowers and how to adhere them to a surface using PVA glue (see working instructions in the example chapter).

Be sure to have the colorful ceramic that you want to work with prepared in advance.

For your safety, put on your eye goggles before cutting the ceramic to protect your eyes from small ceramic shards.

I recommend you to start with ceramic that is a little softer than others for your first mosaic piece, for easier cutting. After you've gotten comfortable, then you can start working with different tiles grades.

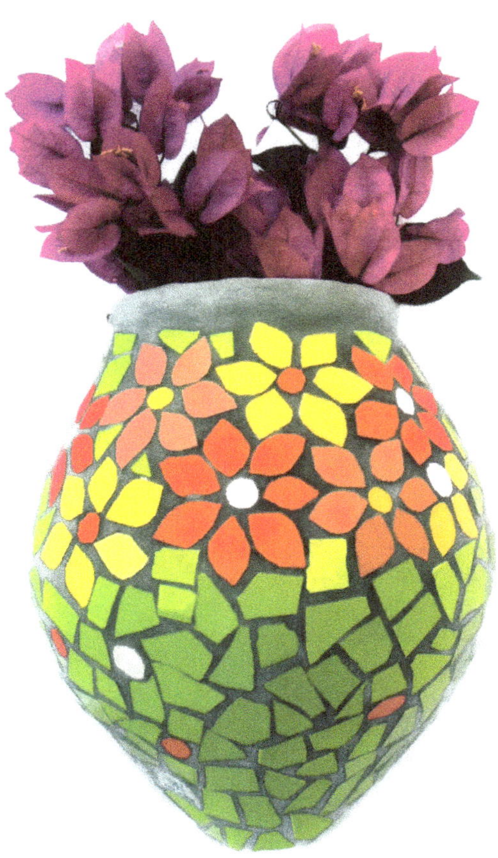

Using the mosaic cutter

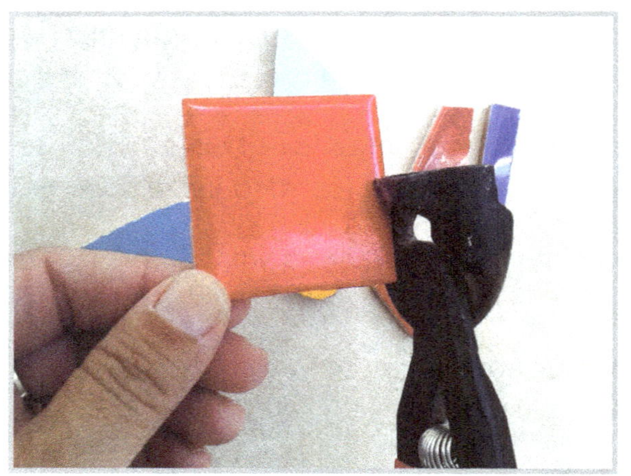

Hold the bottom of the cutter with your dominant hand, having the curved side facing towards the ceramics. Hold the ceramic tile in your non-dominant hand, and in the other one, hold the bottom of the cutter handle.

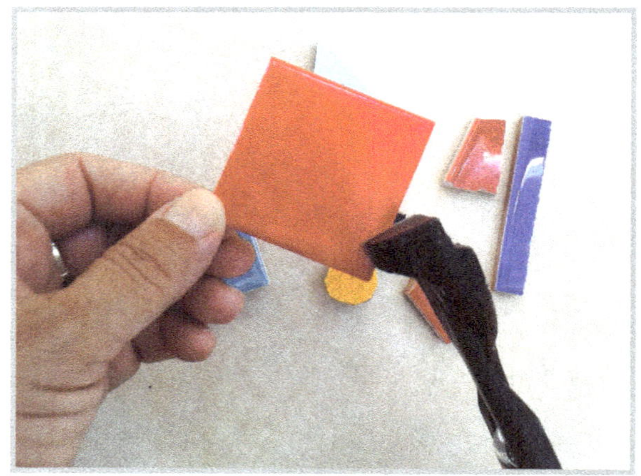

Hold the ceramic tile with the cutter in a straight or diagonal direction to suit the type of crop you want, and clip!

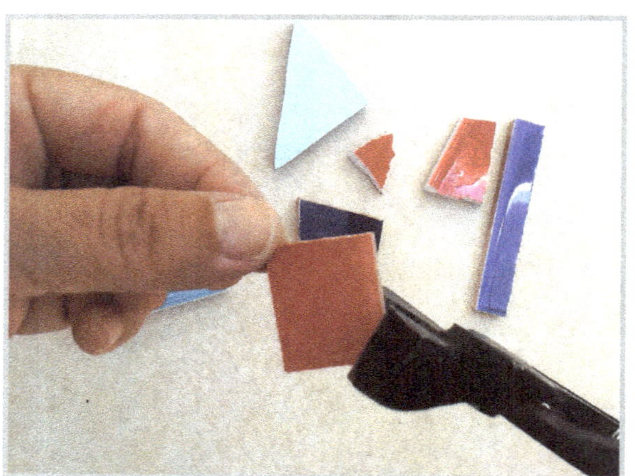

If you want to cut small pieces or to shape the tile, hold the tile by the widest part of the cutter and clip.

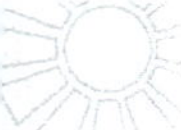

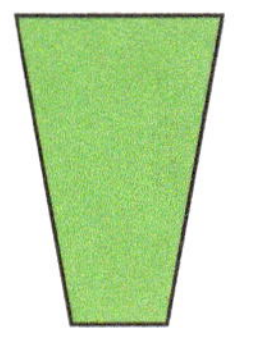

Cutting petals: Cone petals

This first petal is very simple to cut, with 2 finishing options for your choice. As you will see in this book, all the petals are made from a basic shape.

1 Cut the ceramic to a rectangular shape according to the appropriate flower petal size.

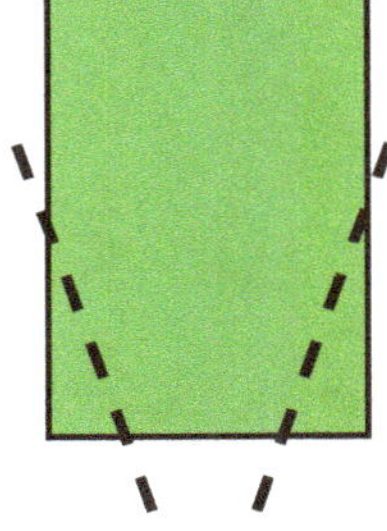

2 Now cut diagonally the two lower corners of the rectangle as shown in the example.

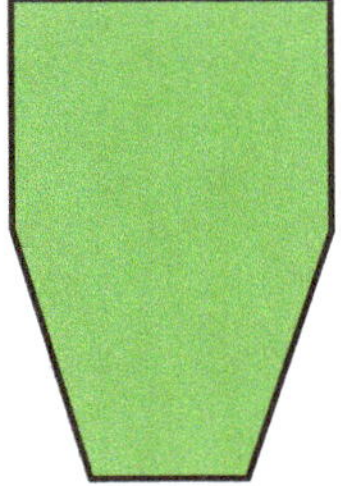

3 You will get a shape similar to the above.

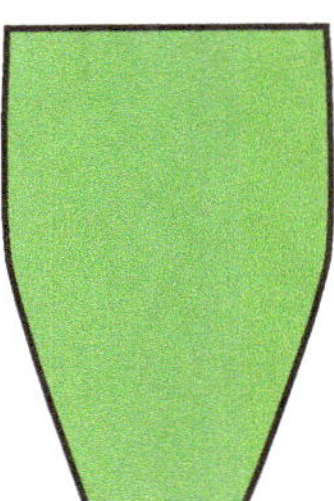

4 Just one more step: round the sharp external corners, making fine cuts (do it with the wide side of the cutter). Your leaf is ready!

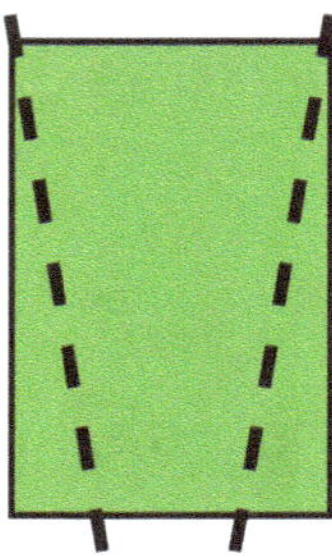

5 Another version for this petal: cut two triangles from the rectangle as shown in the example (with the wide side of the cutter)

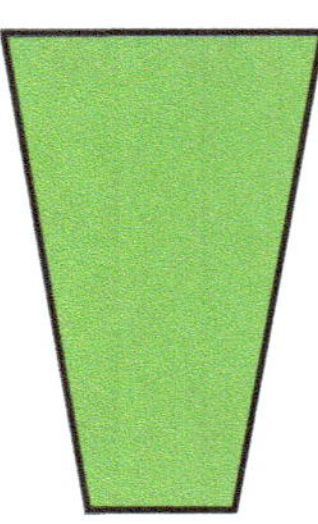

6 That's it! Your first leaf is ready!

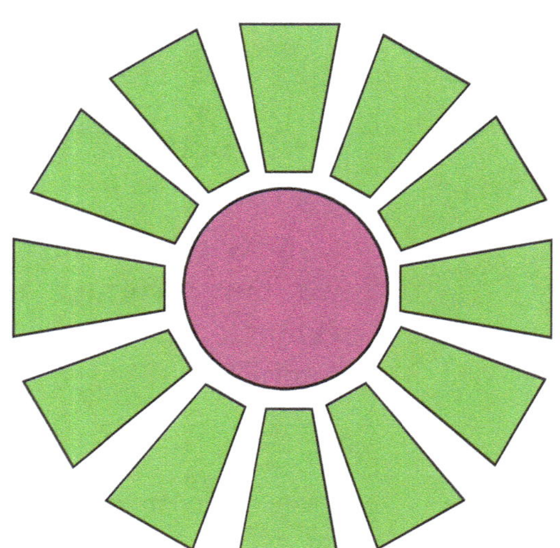

7 To make a flower place a ceramic or a glass nugget circle in the middle, arranging the cut leaves around it.

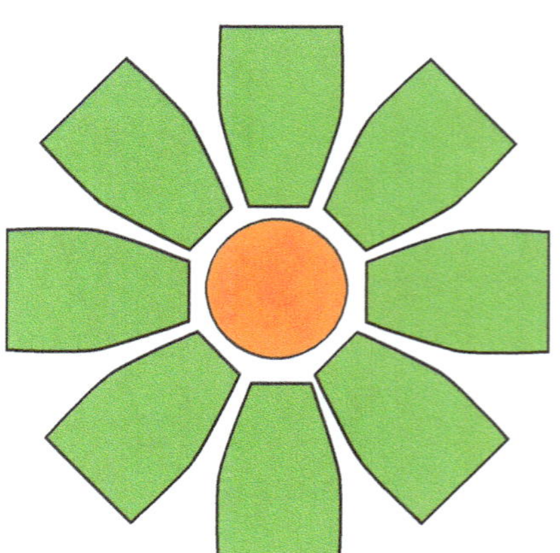

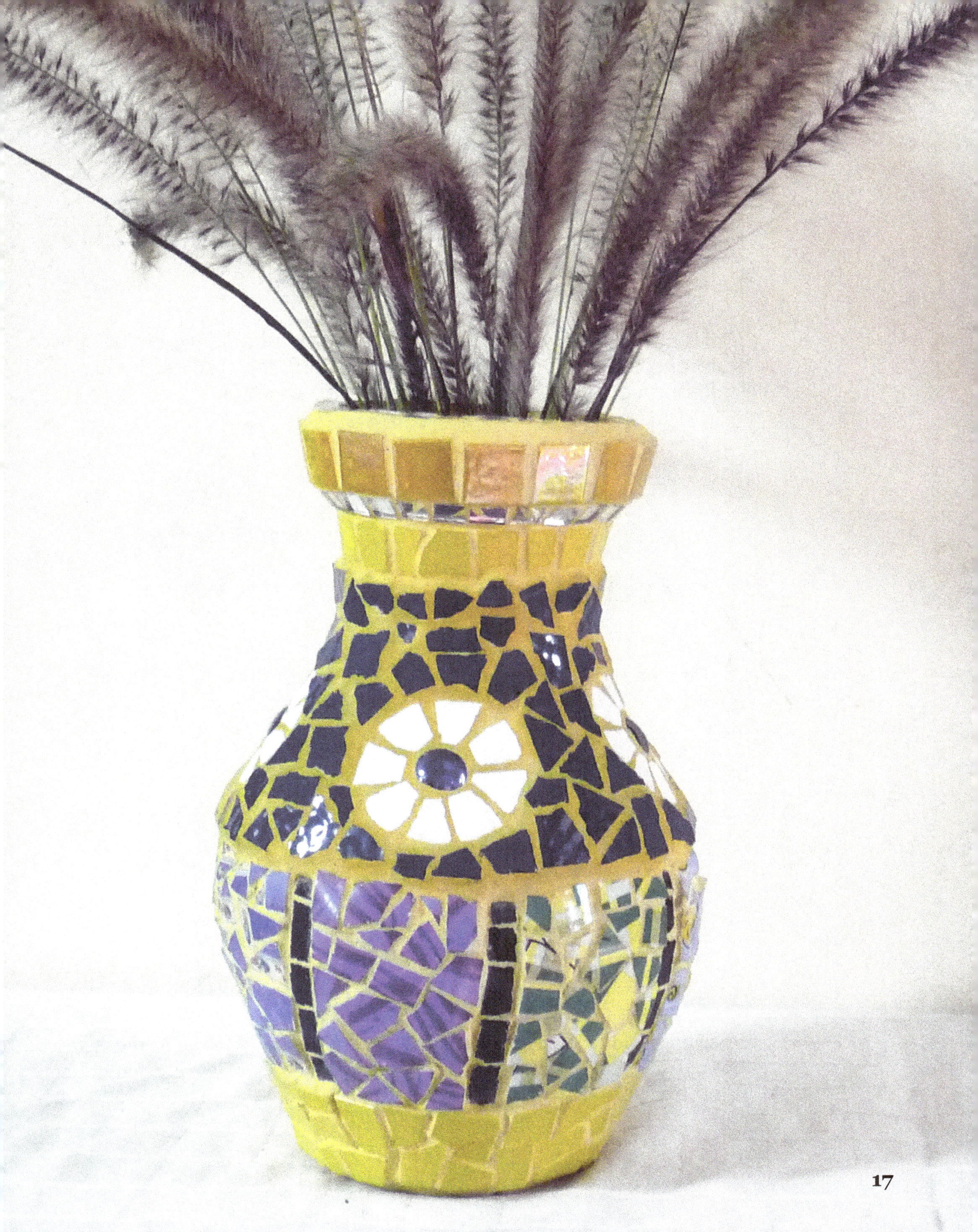

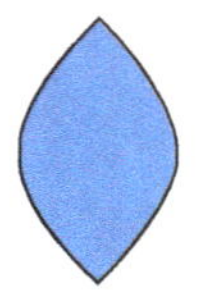

Cutting petals:
Sharp petal shape

In this chapter we will learn how to cut pointy petals to create a flower like a sunflower.

It is not difficult; we will learn the technique of cutting petals similar to one another. Follow the instructions and they will lead you through creating the perfect petal step by step!

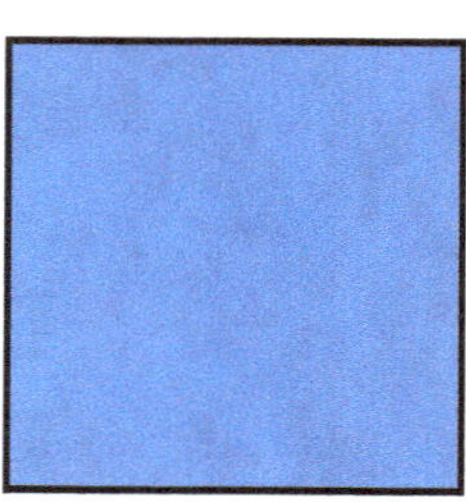

1 Cut the ceramic to square according to the appropriate petal size for your flower.

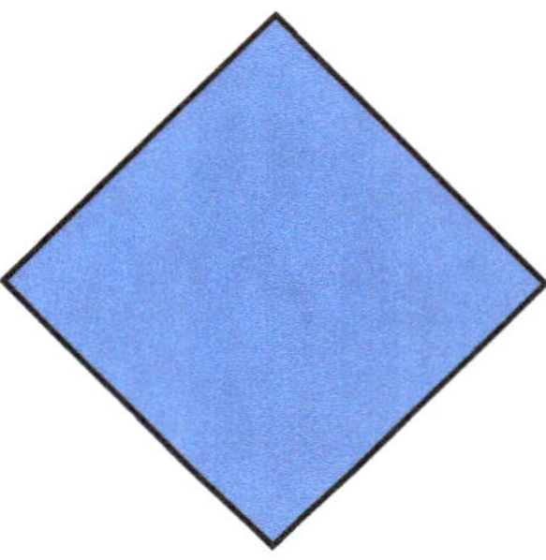

2 Turn the square 45 degrees, pointed tip up.

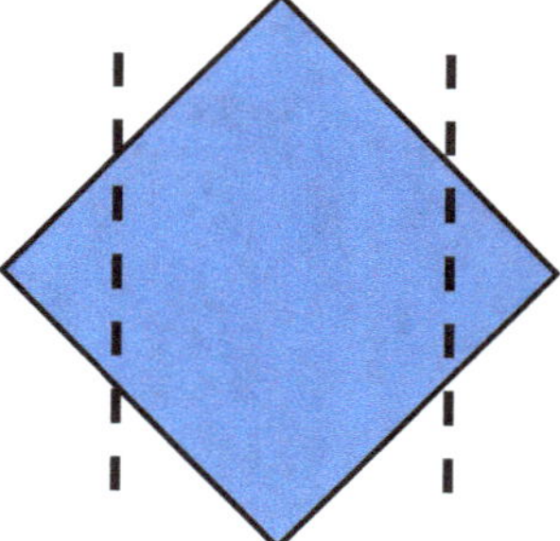

3 Cut 2 small triangles off the tips of two opposite edges.

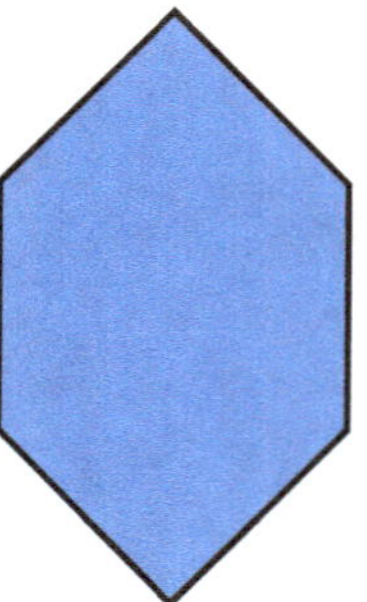

4 Continue to round the edges of the triangles created after cutting.

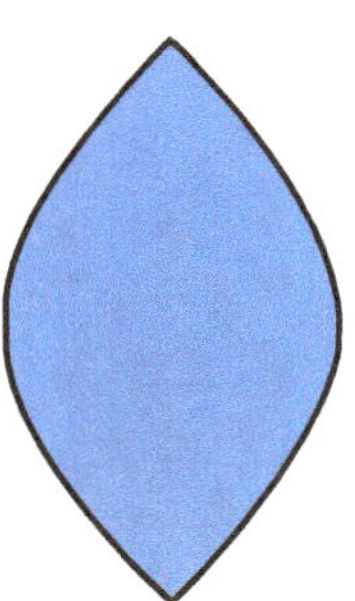

5 You have the perfect petal! Keep going with the extra petals to create a complete flower.

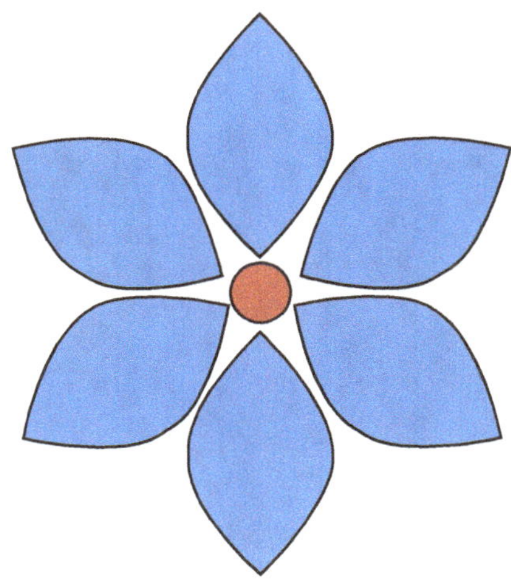

6 You will need 5-6 petals for a small flower.

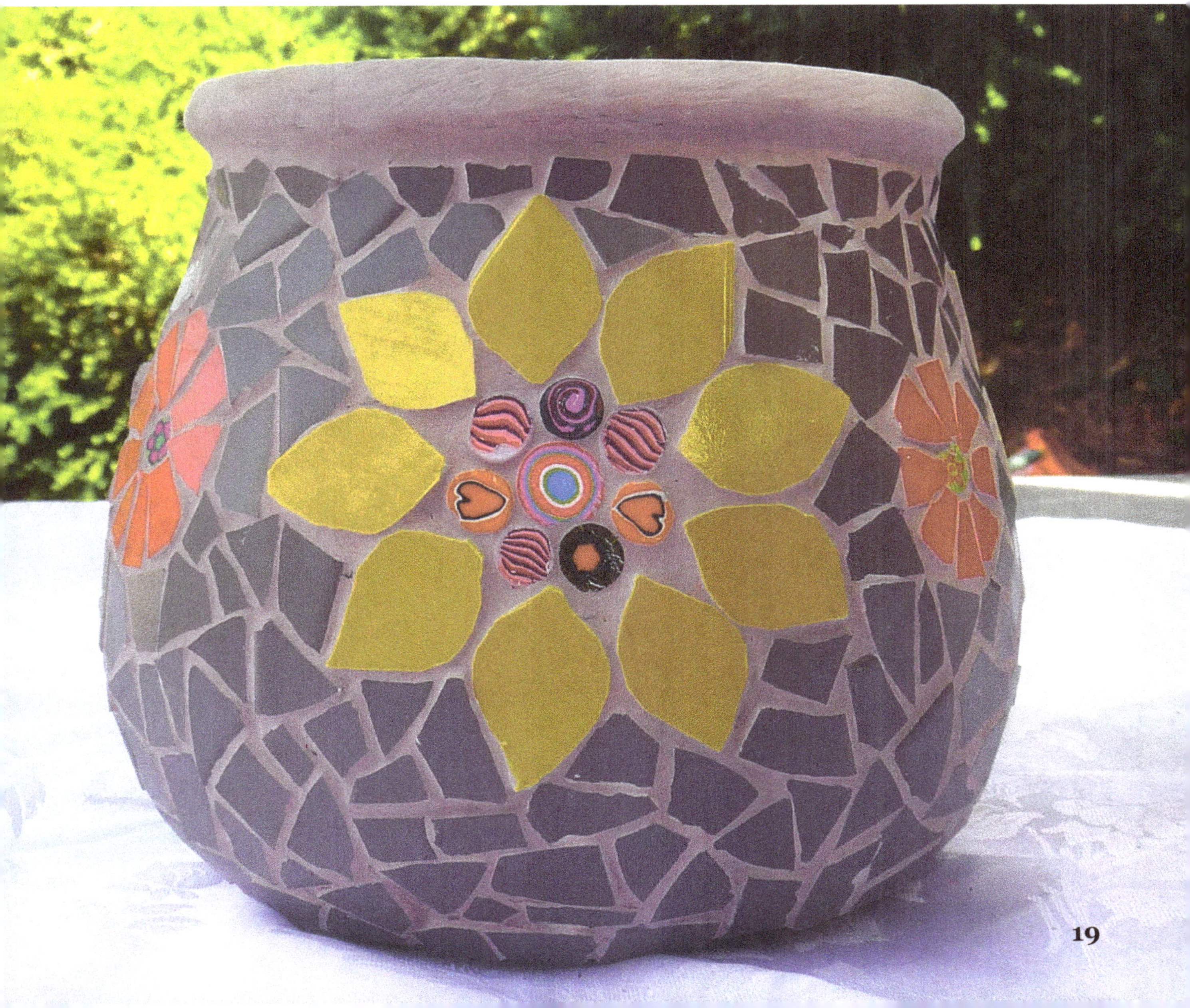

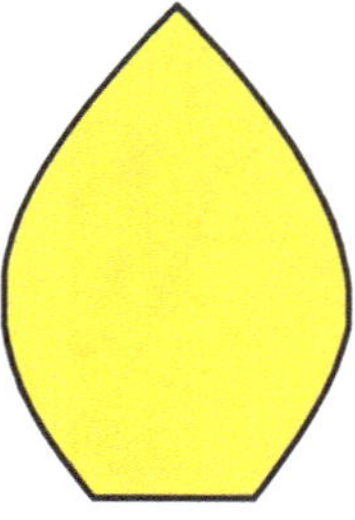

7 For making a sunflower you have to cut the bottom corner off the original petal you created.

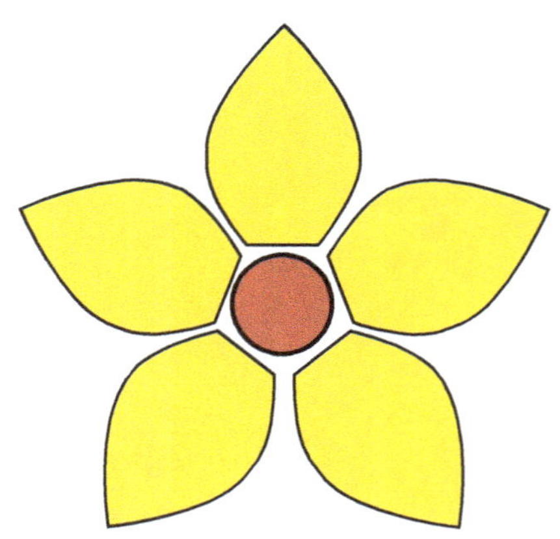

8 One edge of each of your petals should be flat, and the side opposite the flat one should be pointed.

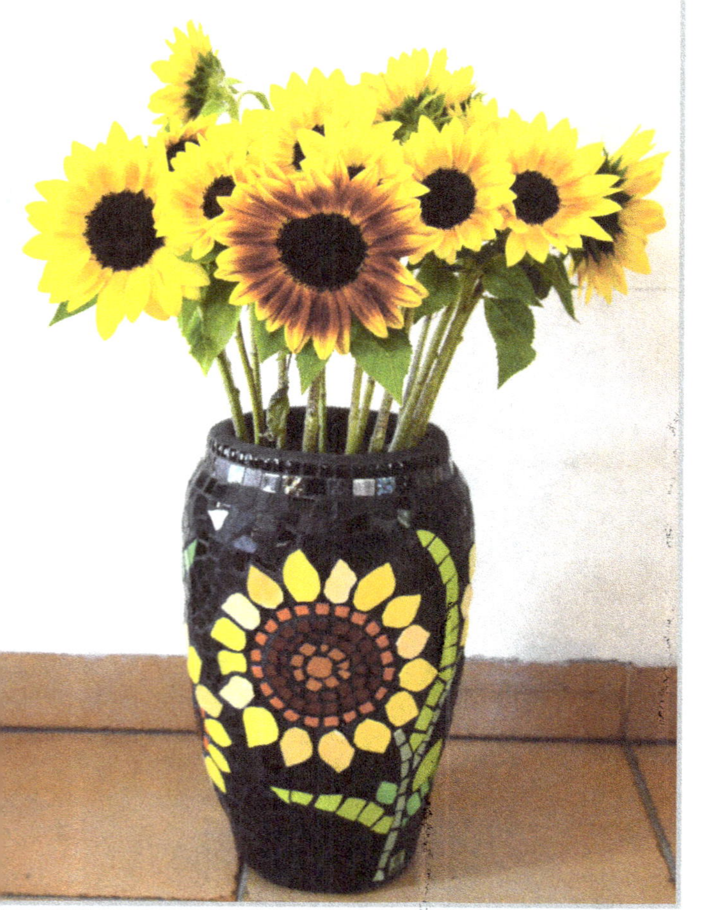

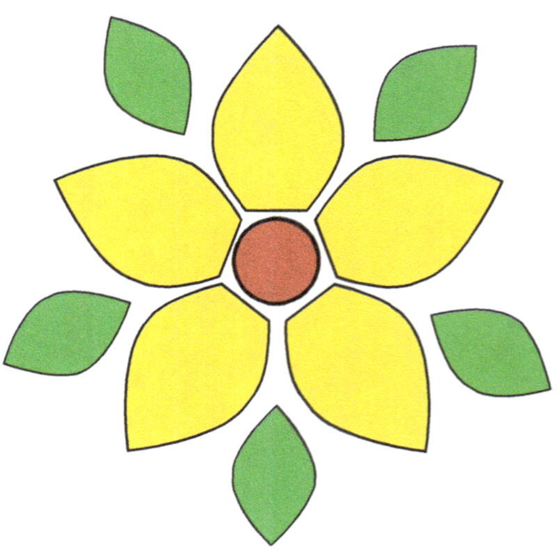

9 You can use this form as well for green leaves and connect them around the flower you have created

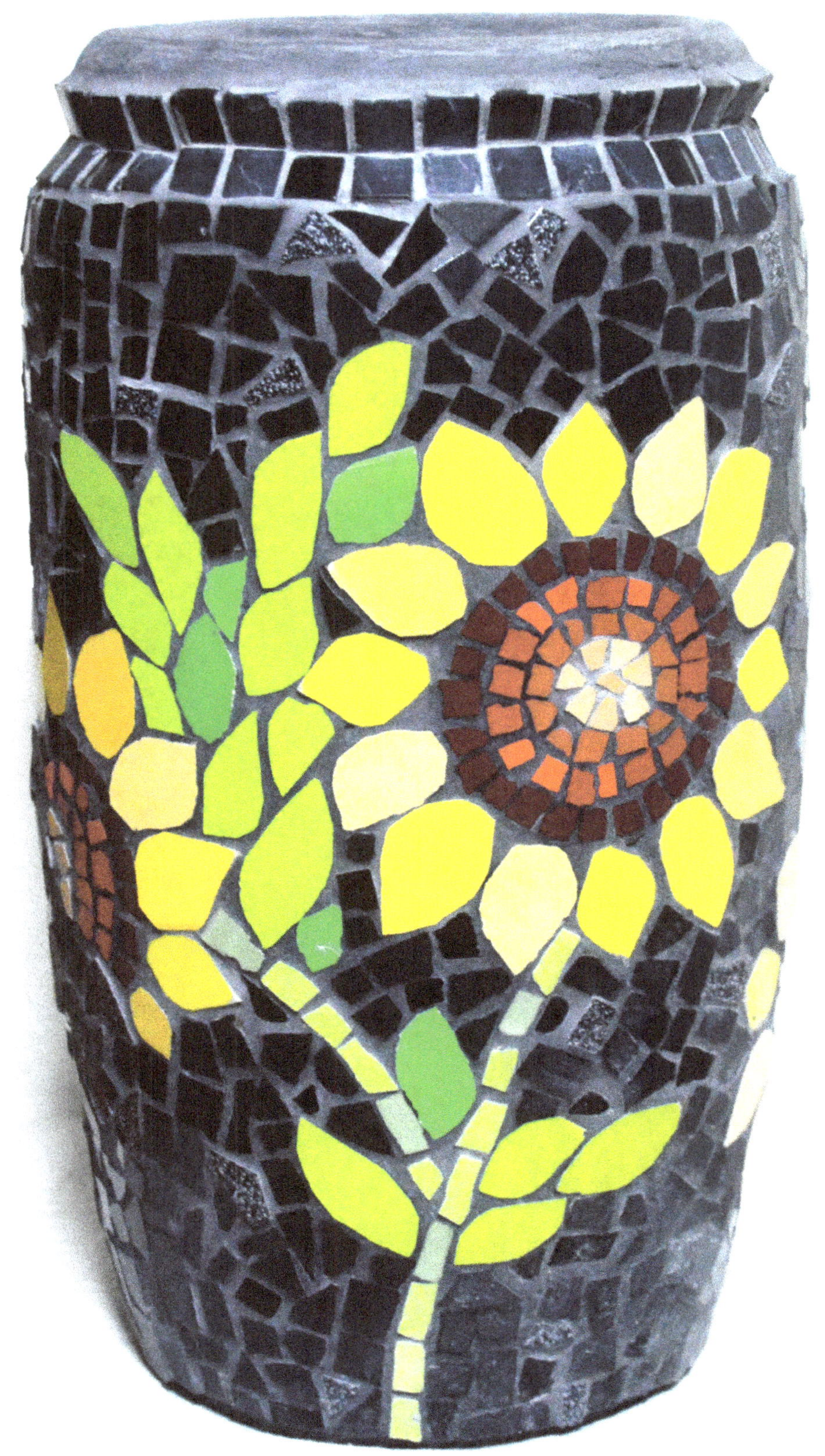

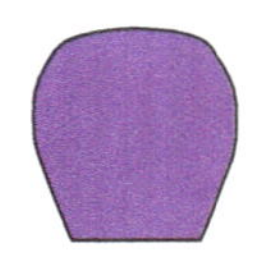

Cutting petals:
Rounded petals

Like the previous petals we have created, here we also begin with a small square tile.

This is the same technique, with a slight change in the end that creates a round petal shape.

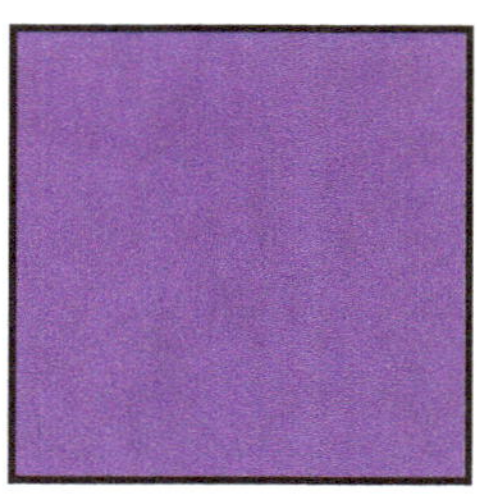

1 Cut the ceramic into a square according to the appropriate flower petal size.

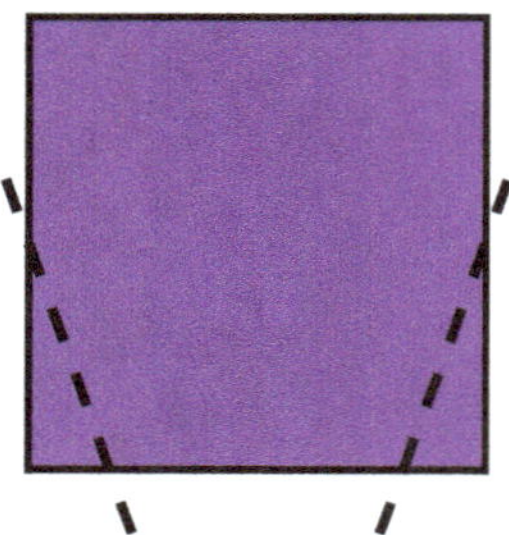

2 Now cut the two lower corners of the square on a diagonal as the example shows.

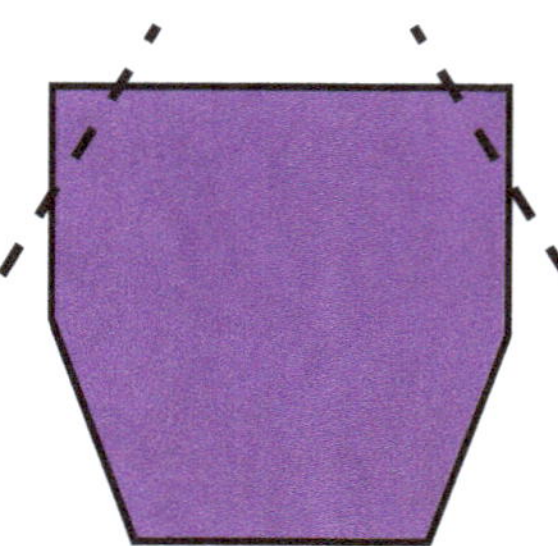

3 Cut just the tips off the top corners.

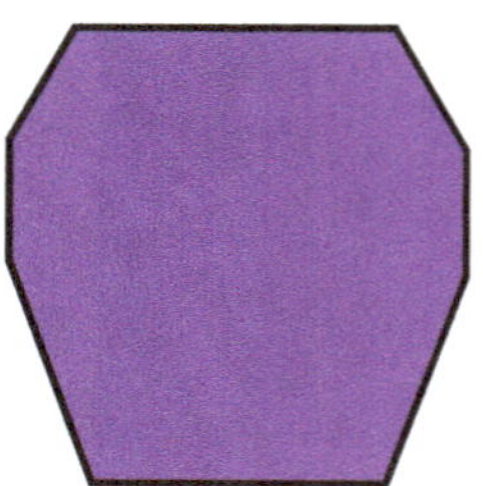

4 At this point you have to round the sharp corners, making fine cuts around the edges of the tile (do it with the wide side of the cutter).

5 Now you have a nice round petal! Continue to cut more petals to create a flower.

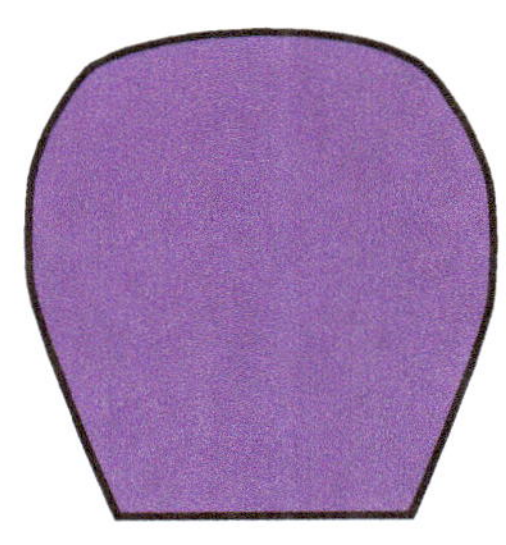

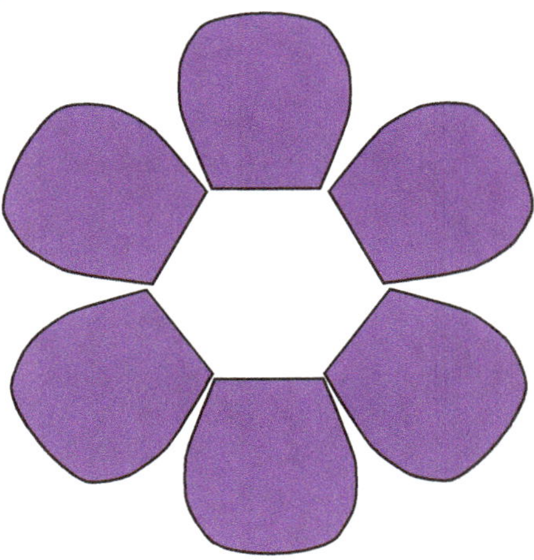

6 Voila! Your finished mosaic flower.

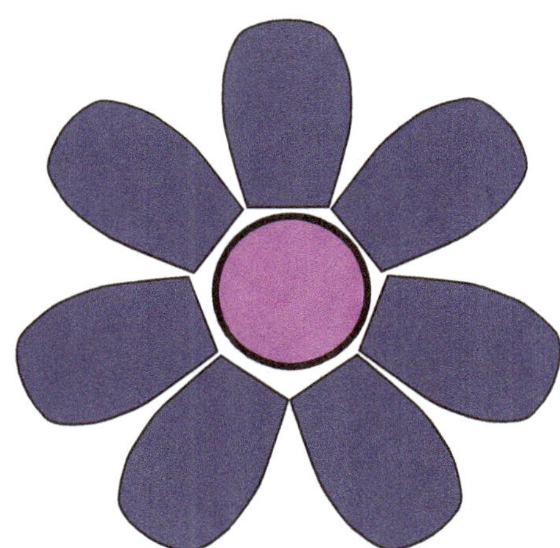

7 To create narrow petals, simply start the process with a rectangular tile instead of a square one.

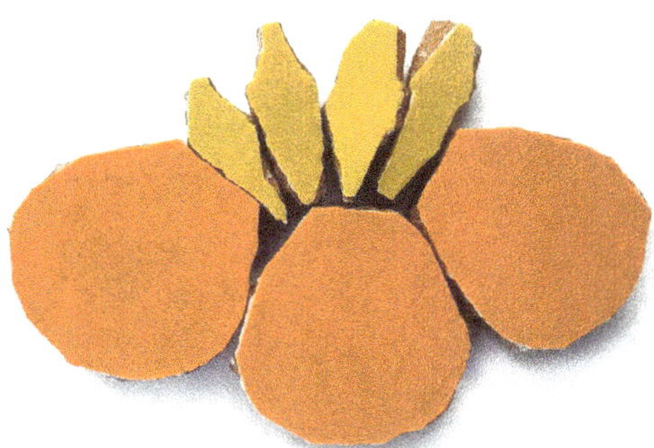

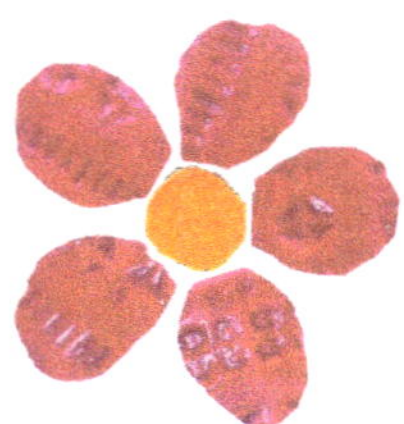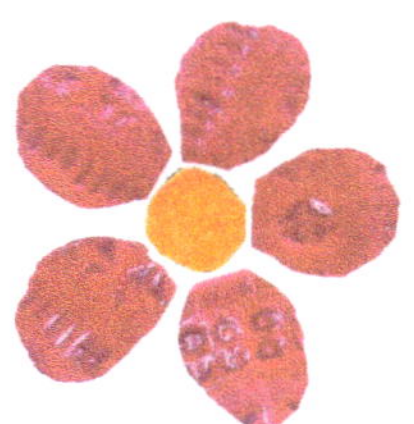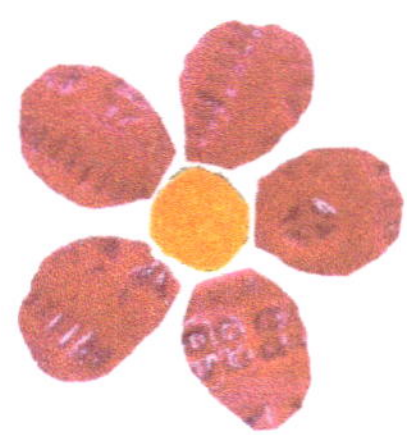

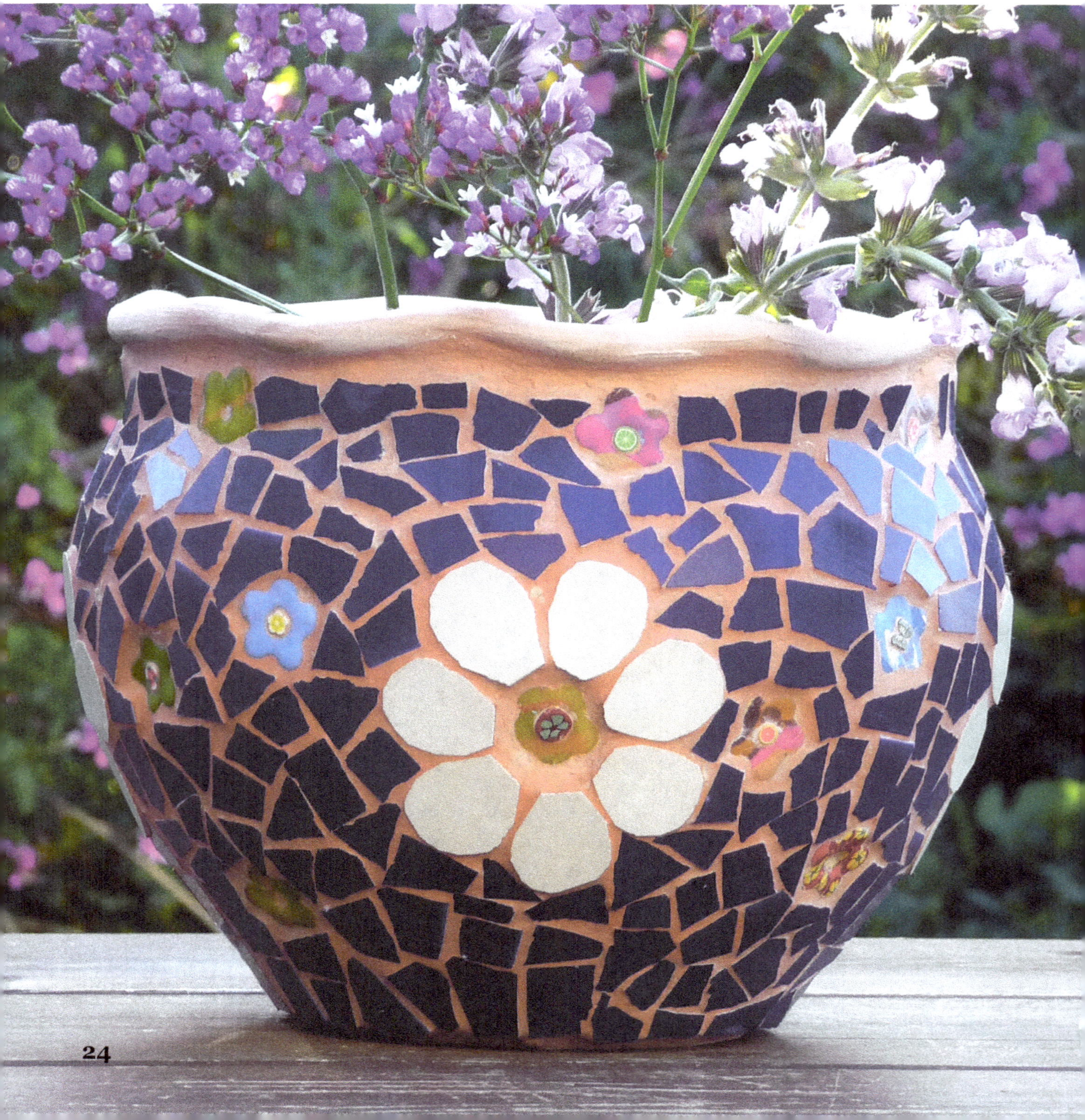

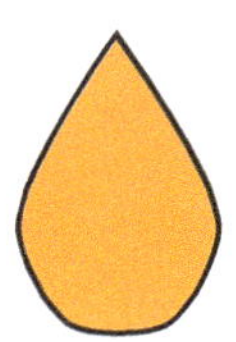

Cutting petals:
Drop-shaped petals

For these petals we will use ceramics cut to triangular shapes. To create one flower we use 6-8 petals, depending on the center size.

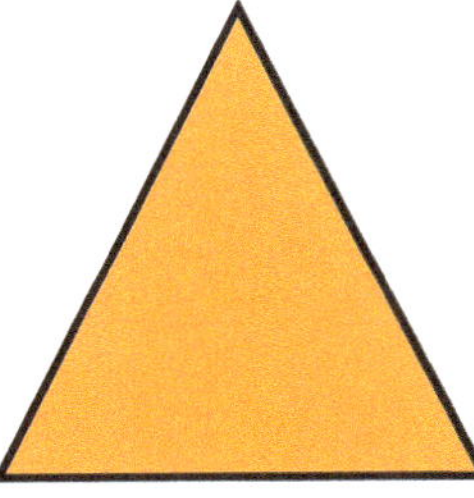

1 Cut your ceramic to a triangle according to the appropriate flower petal size.

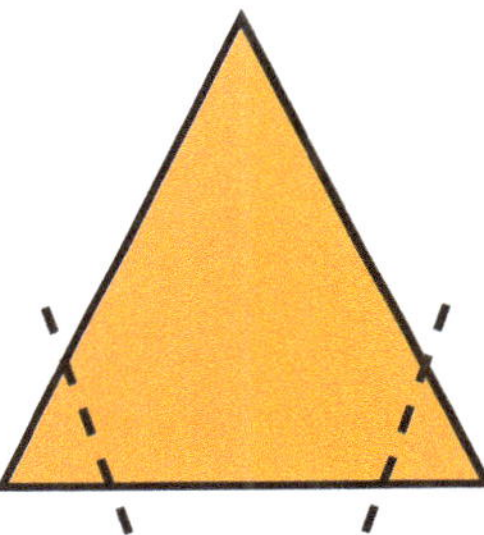

2 Cut the two bottom corners of the triangle.

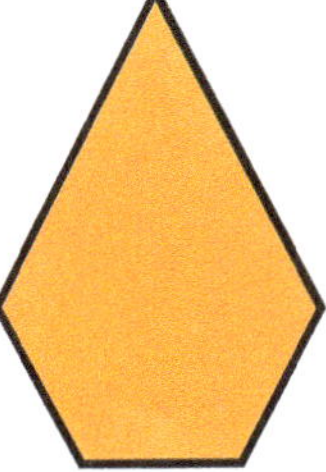

3 Now you only have to round the angular edges along the bottom...

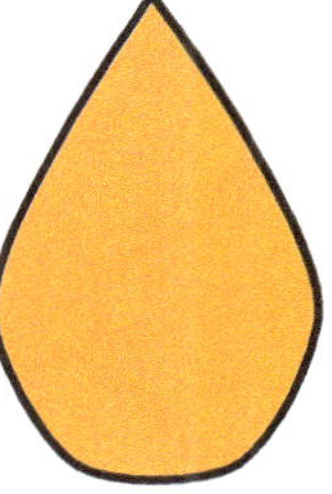

4 ...and you have created a beautiful drop-shaped petal!

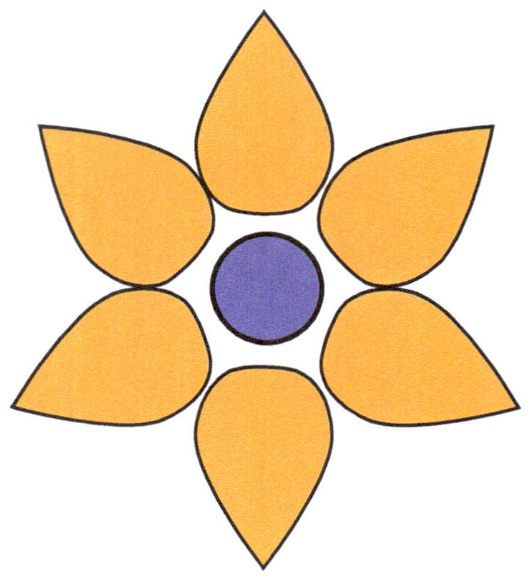

5 Create the flower: put a round tile or a glass bead in the center, arrange the petals around it.

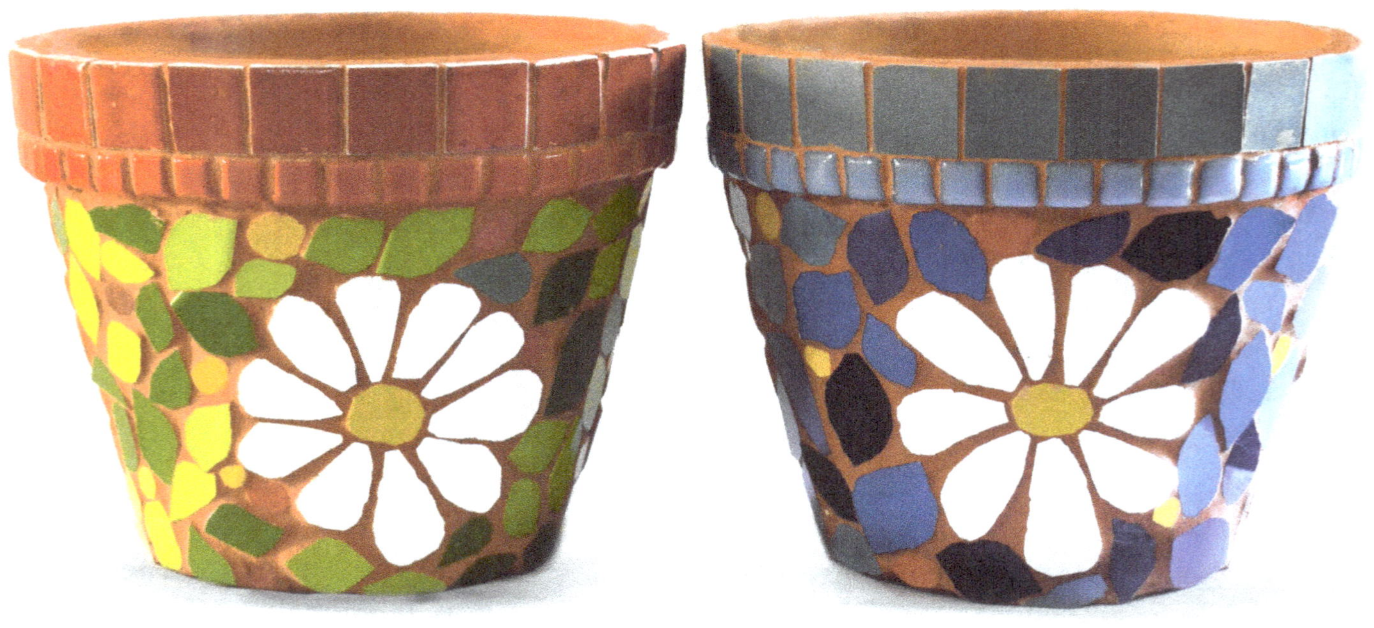

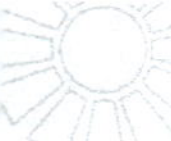

6 You can reverse the direction of the petals with the point inward, creating a flower without the circle in the center.

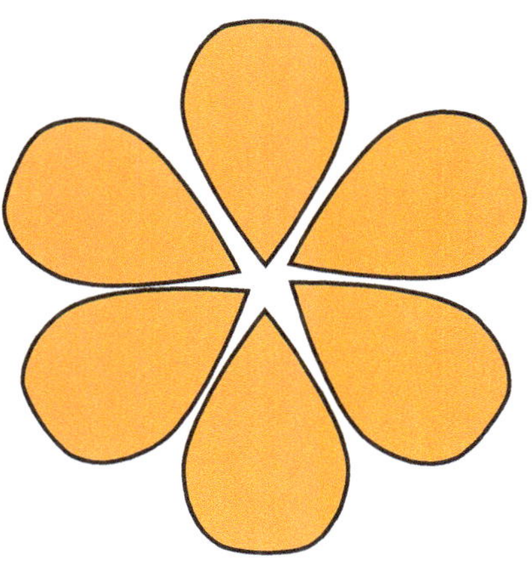

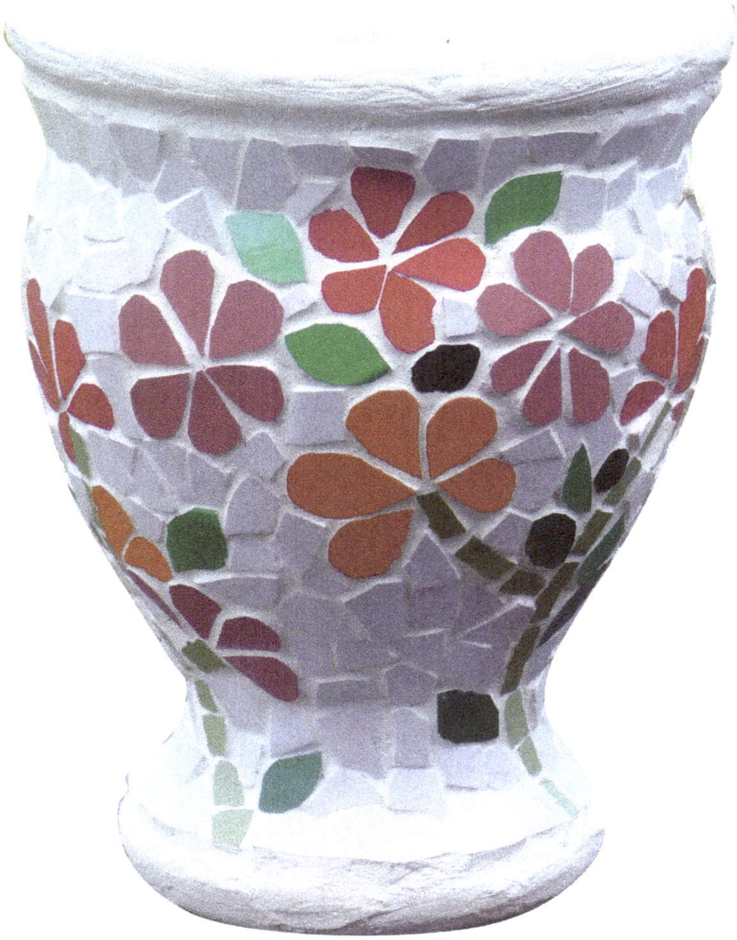

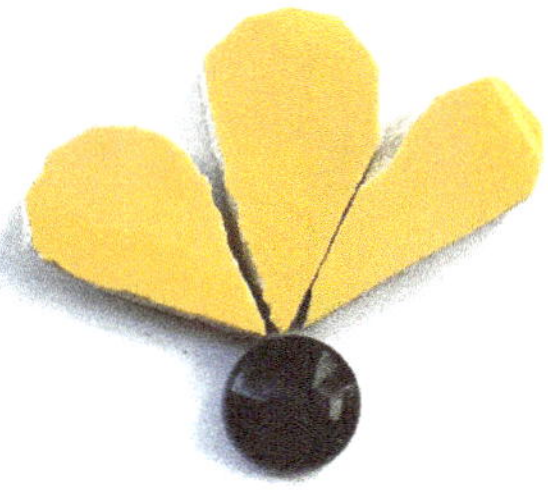

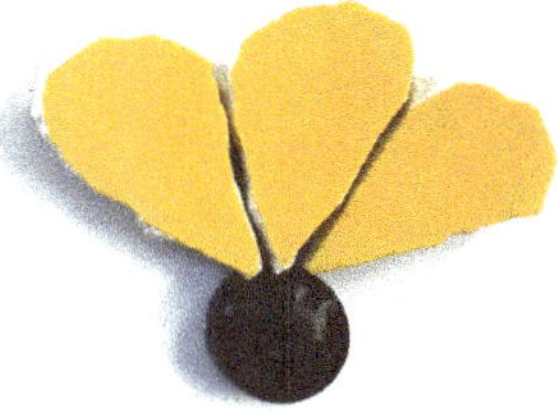

Cutting petals: Rose

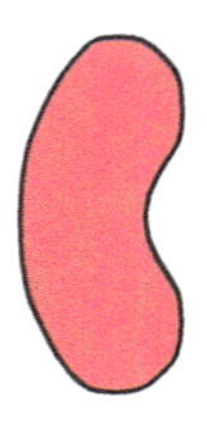

The rose is the most complicated flower, but after practicing with the previous cutting techniques it won't seem so hard. Again, this is a technique that is learned gradually.

The rose consists of three parts:

a. A circle in the center, which will be cut from a square like the petals we learned earlier.

b. Bean-shaped petals, which are cut from rectangular tiles.

c. Rose end petals, also cut from rectangular tiles.

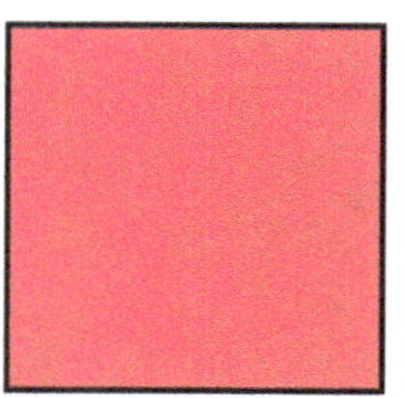

1 Cut the ceramic to a square to create the flower center.

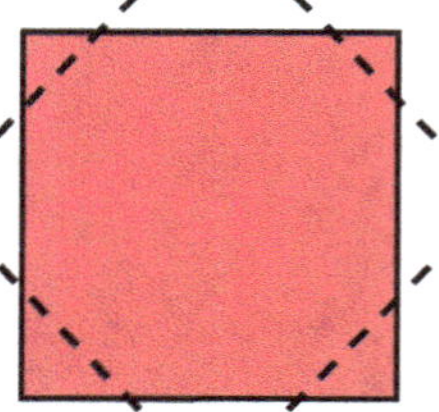

2 Cut the four corners off with your cutter.

3 Continue to round the shape created by finely cutting of all triangular corners with the wide part of the cutter.

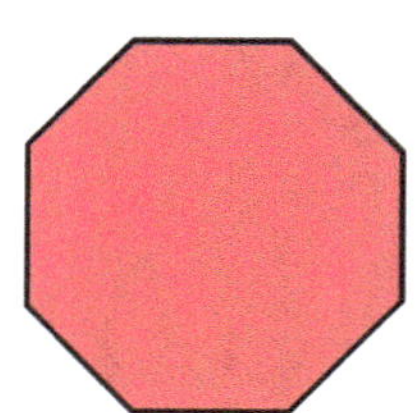

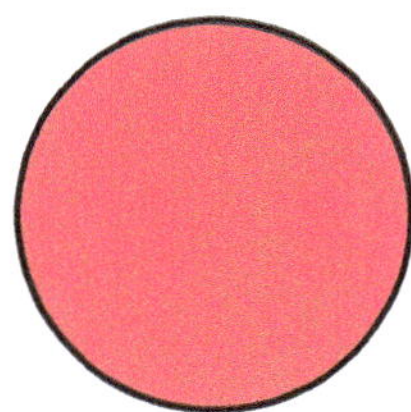

4 You have formed a circle - this will be the flower's center.

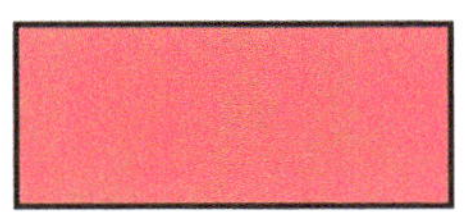

5 The flower petals will be created from rectangular tiles.

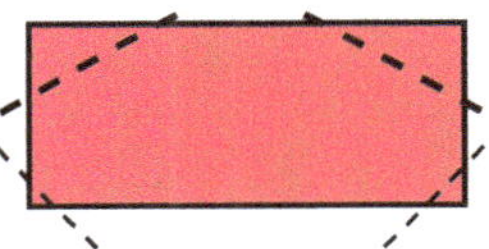

6 Cut their corners off in the style shown.

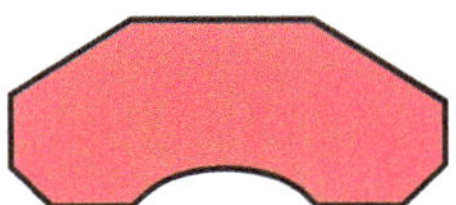

7 Round the sharp corners and apply further cutting in the middle to create an arc shape.

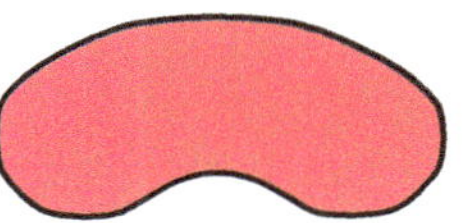

8 Round the petal from all sides. Make about 12-15 more petals; the shape does not have to be precise. Cut the outside rose petals straight on their bottom edge for a circular effect.

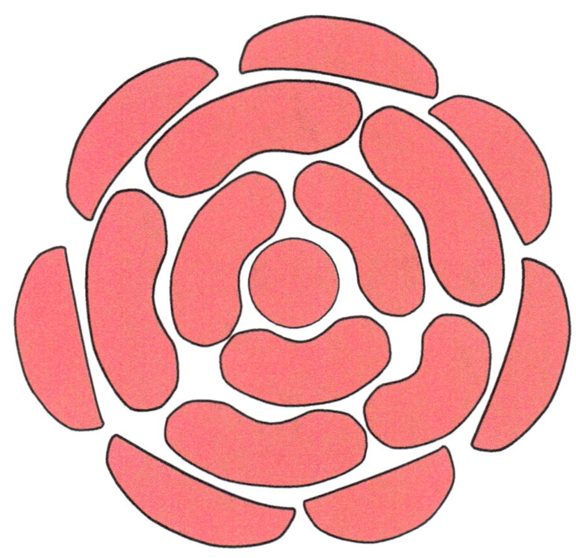

9 Now it's time to make the rose: put the circle in the center, arrange the petals around it as follows.

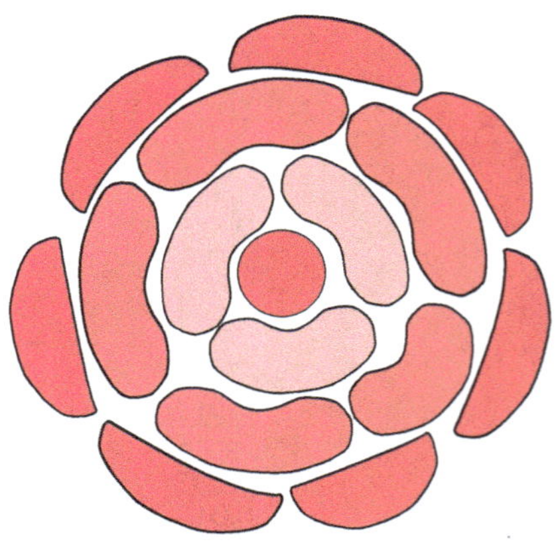

10 For a rich variety of the flower, you can cut the petals of a rose from two different colors, or highlight the circle center with a contrasting ceramic color.

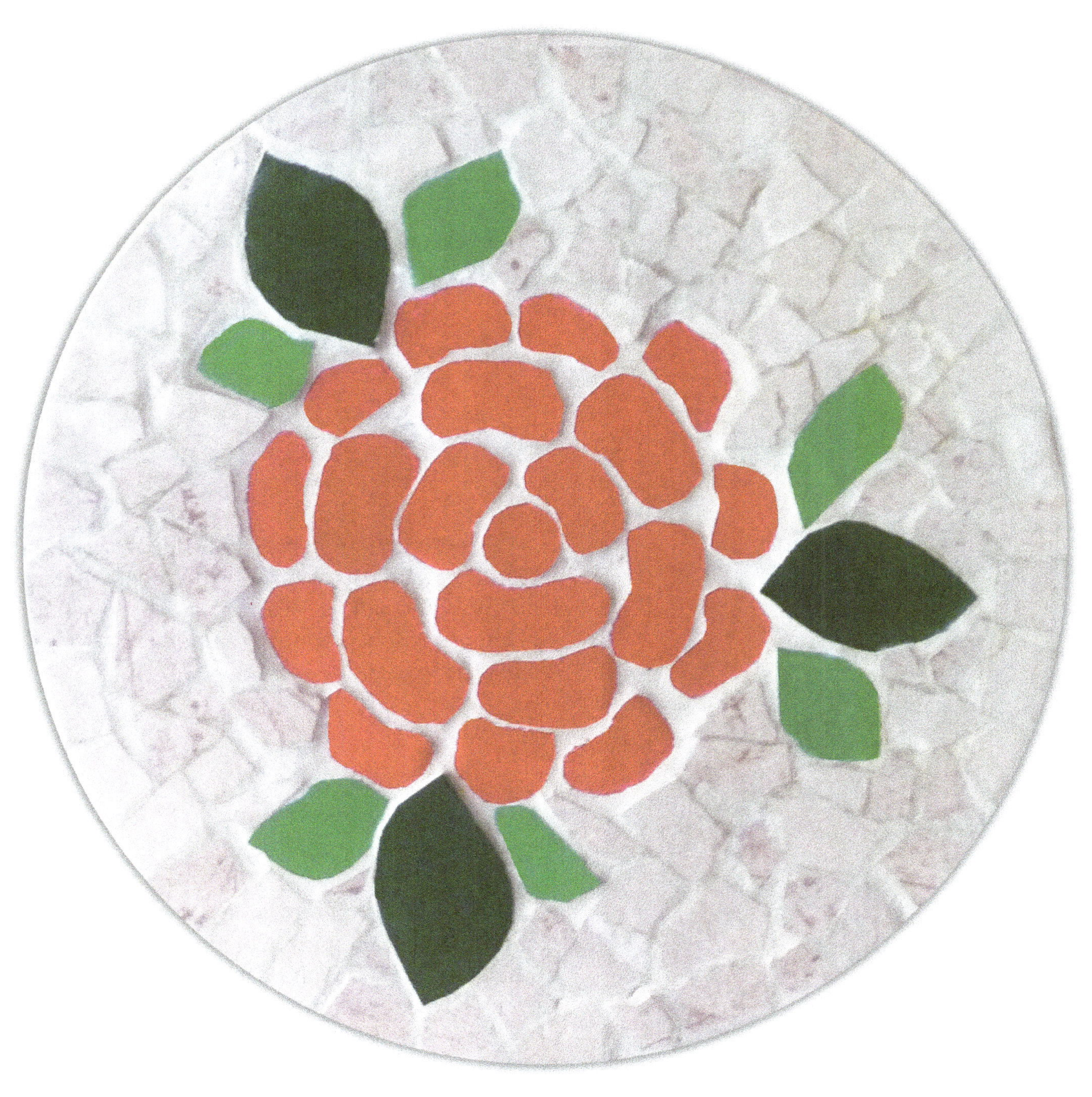

Project sample

Let's take a look at a real example by preparing a base for a pot (can also be used for hanging), with the flower pattern we learned:

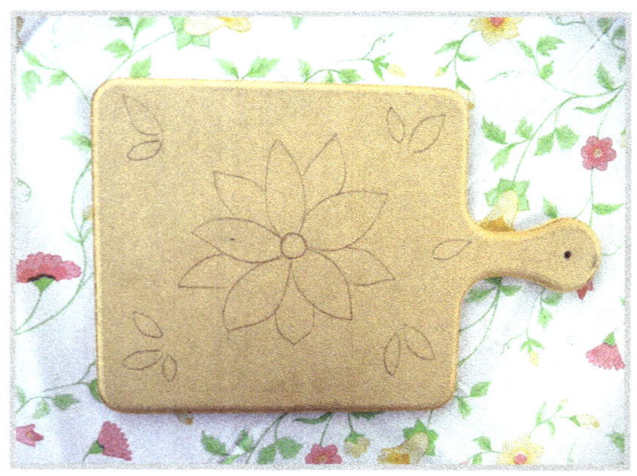

1 Choose the work surface—in this case an MDF board. Plan the design and draw it in with a pencil.

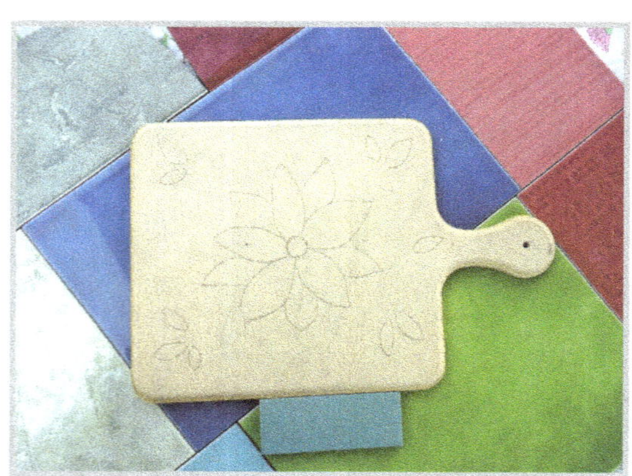

2 Choose the materials for the work–any ceramic colors you want. If you're making a base for a hot pot, notice that all the ceramic you choose will be about the same height to get a smooth surface.

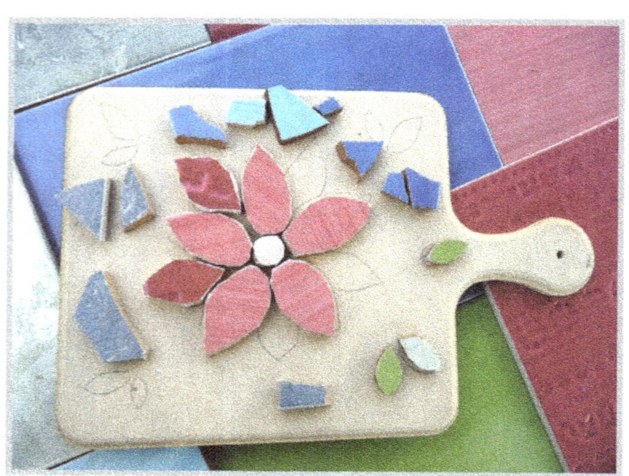

3 Cut the flower petals in any color you wish. Here, I used red and pink. Cut more green leaves in the same way. Cut the background pieces in various shapes from blue ceramic (or the color of your choice). You can cut with mosaic cutter or a hammer.

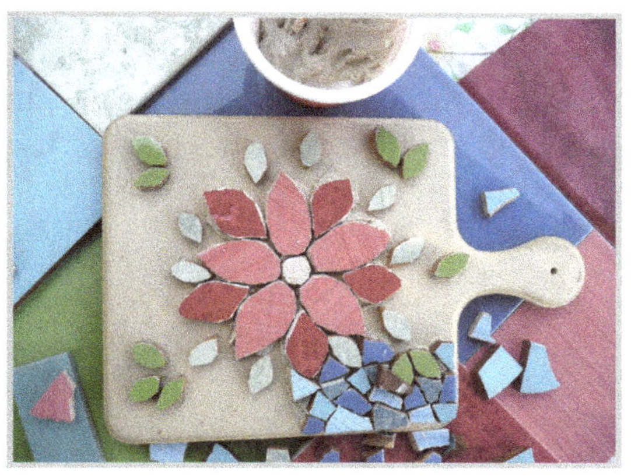

4 Stick the pieces with white glue—first the flower in center of the surface, then the green leaves, and then the rest of the background parts.

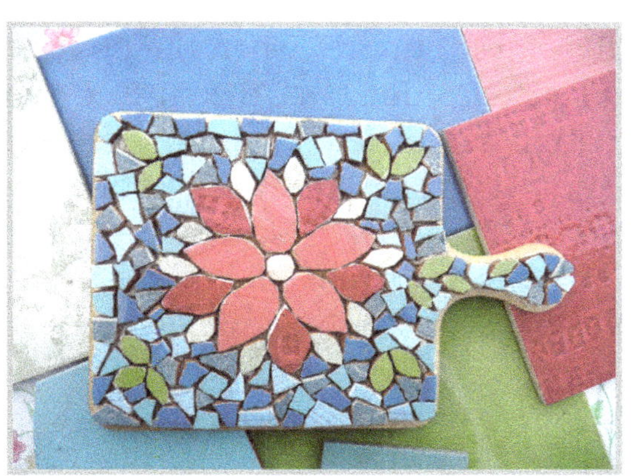

5 Notice that the pieces near the edge are straight and parallel to the frame to create a beautiful finish. IMPORTANT: wait at least 24 hours after gluing before preparing the grout.

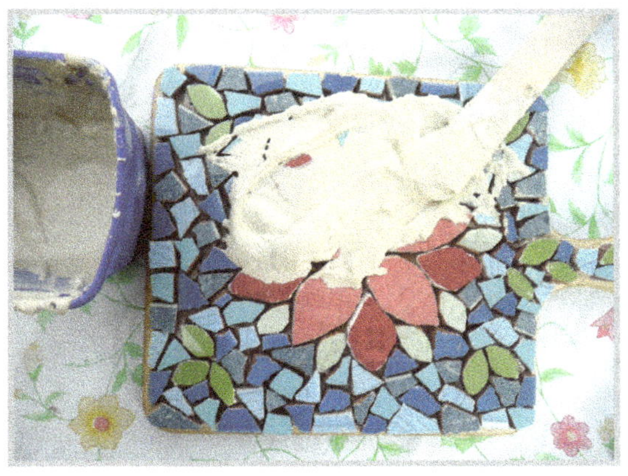

6 Prepare the grout in your desired color (cream in this case). Mix the grout with water in a plastic bowl to the manufacturer's instructions and spread it on the ceramic with a wooden stick until all of the work is covered. You can put an old newspaper under you surface to keep your table clean.

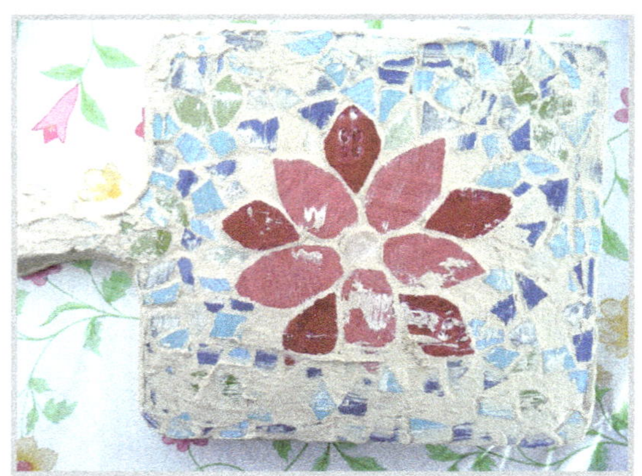

7 Take a small squeegee and spread the grout on the surface until it fills in all slots and holes. Spread the grout around the edges, too, to creating beautiful margins.

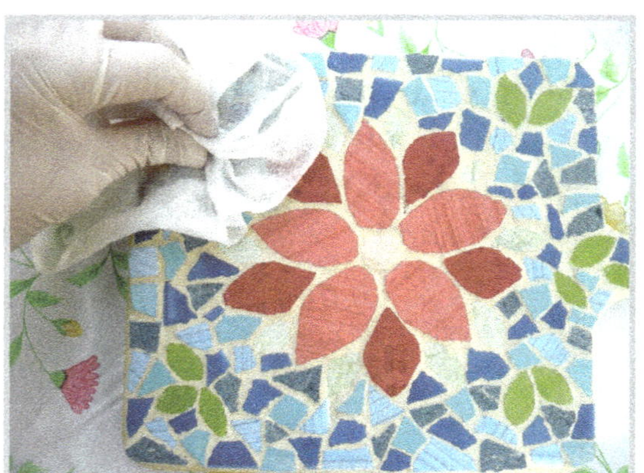

8 After a few minutes when the grout starts to dry, start cleaning: wet the surface using a clean cotton rag or a sponge. Alternate using a wet and dry rag several times until the work is clean. IMPORTANT: Make sure to wet the work. Wetting the grout makes it harder and prevents cracks. Don't skip this step!

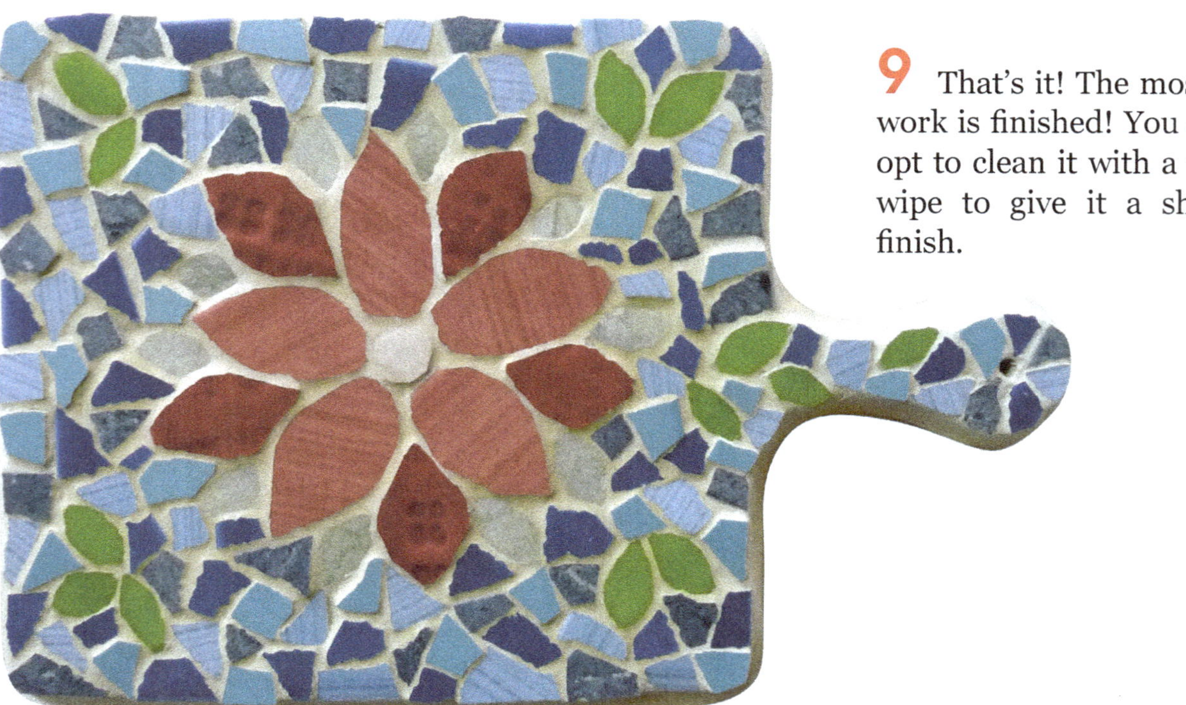

9 That's it! The mosaic work is finished! You can opt to clean it with a wet wipe to give it a shiny finish.

Mosaic flower works

Garden and home Pots

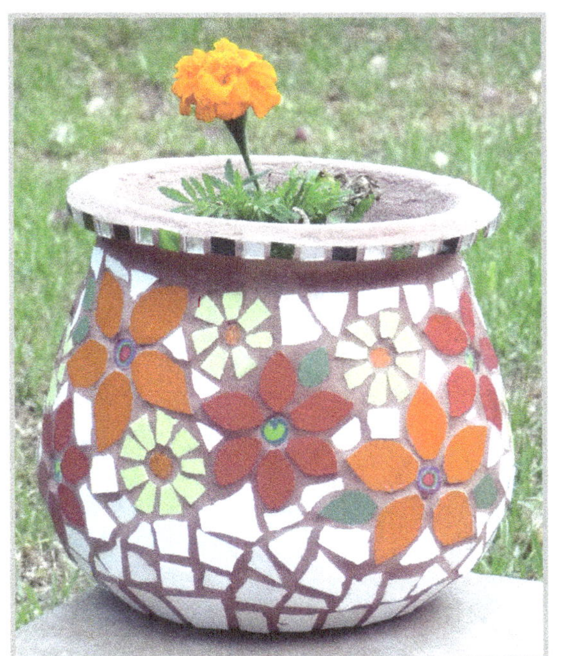

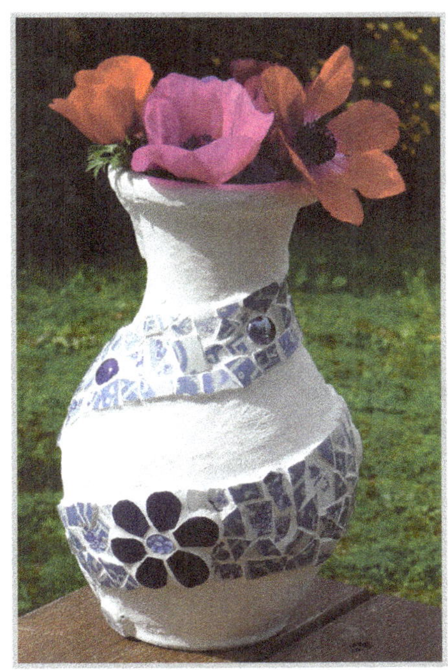

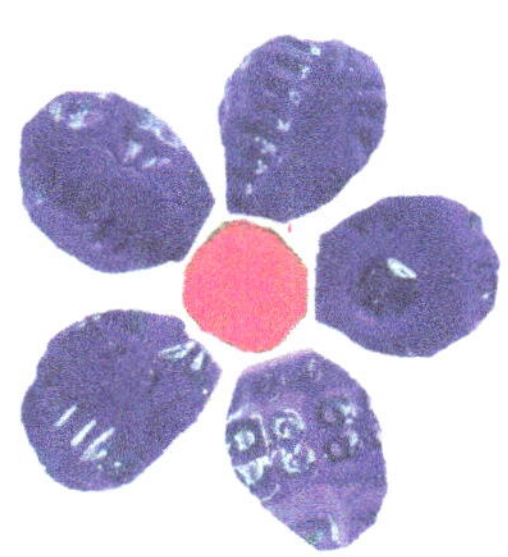

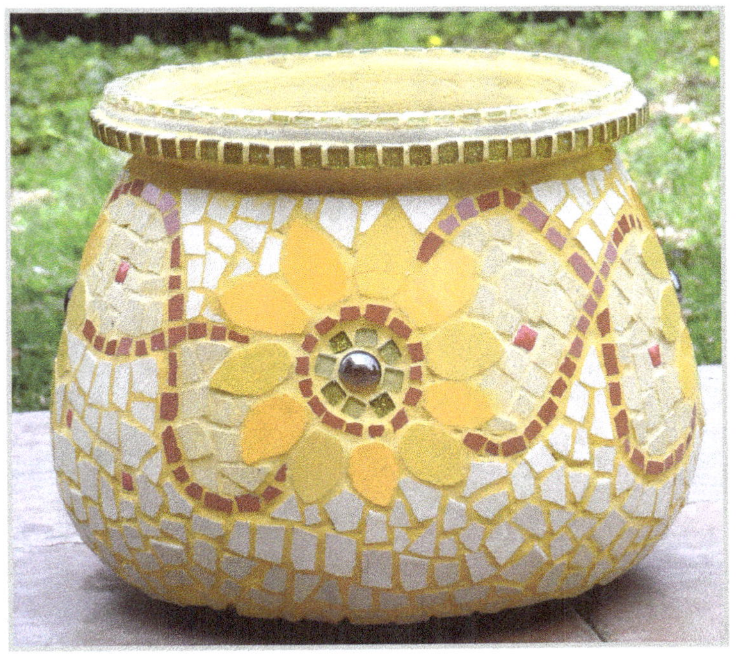

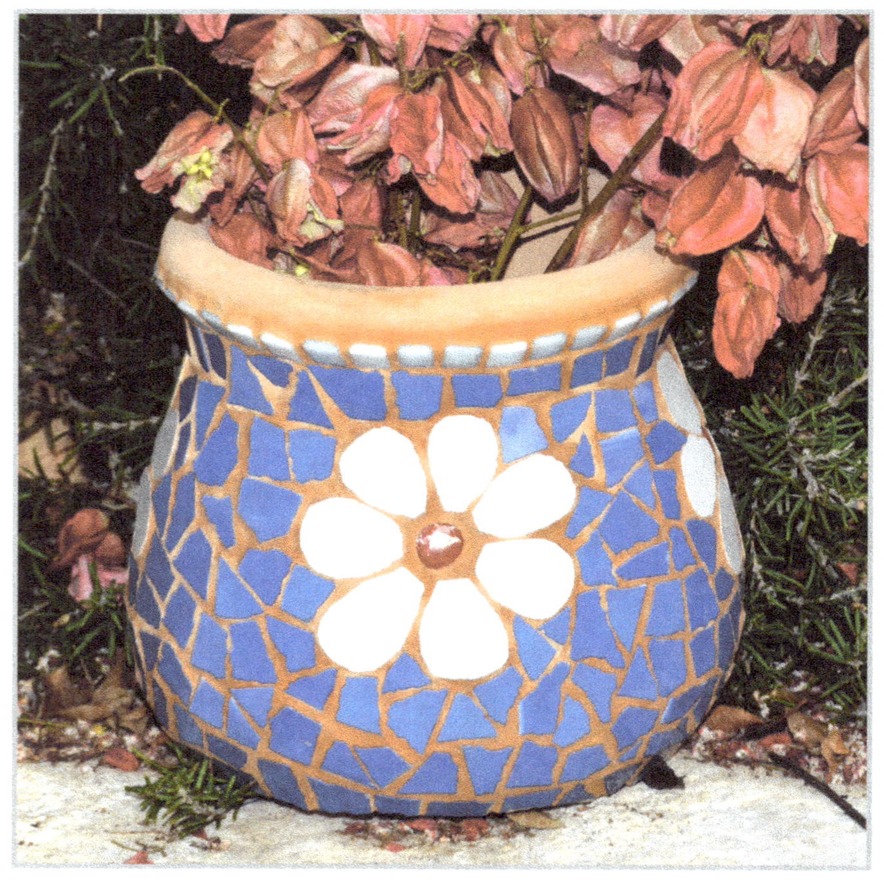

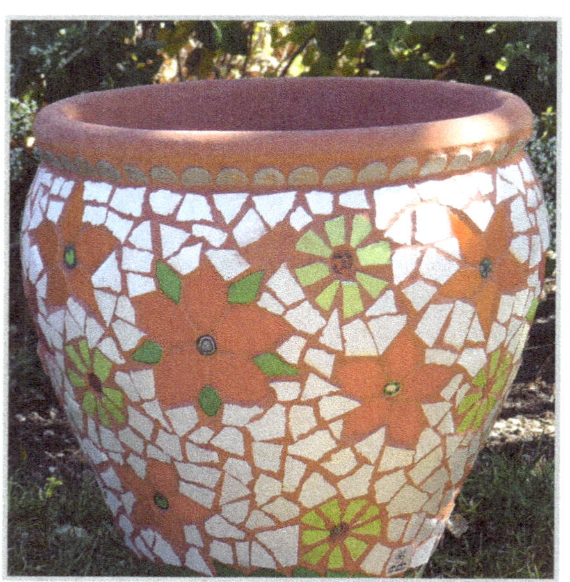

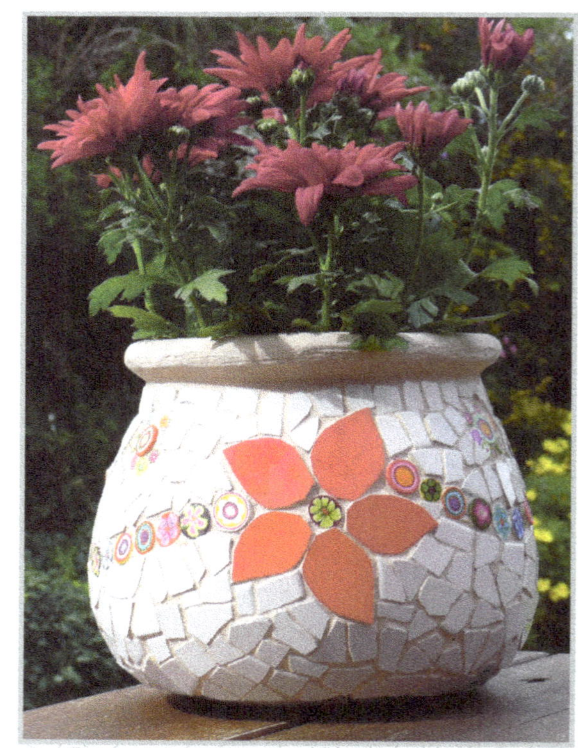

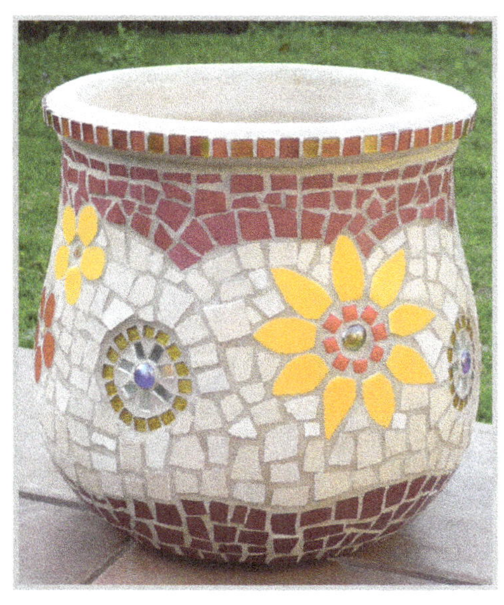

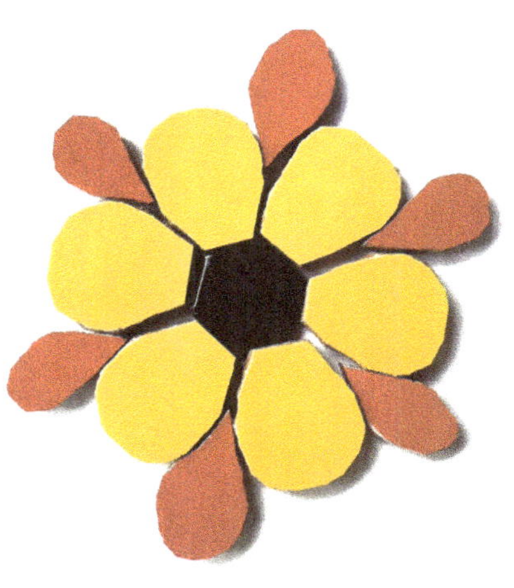

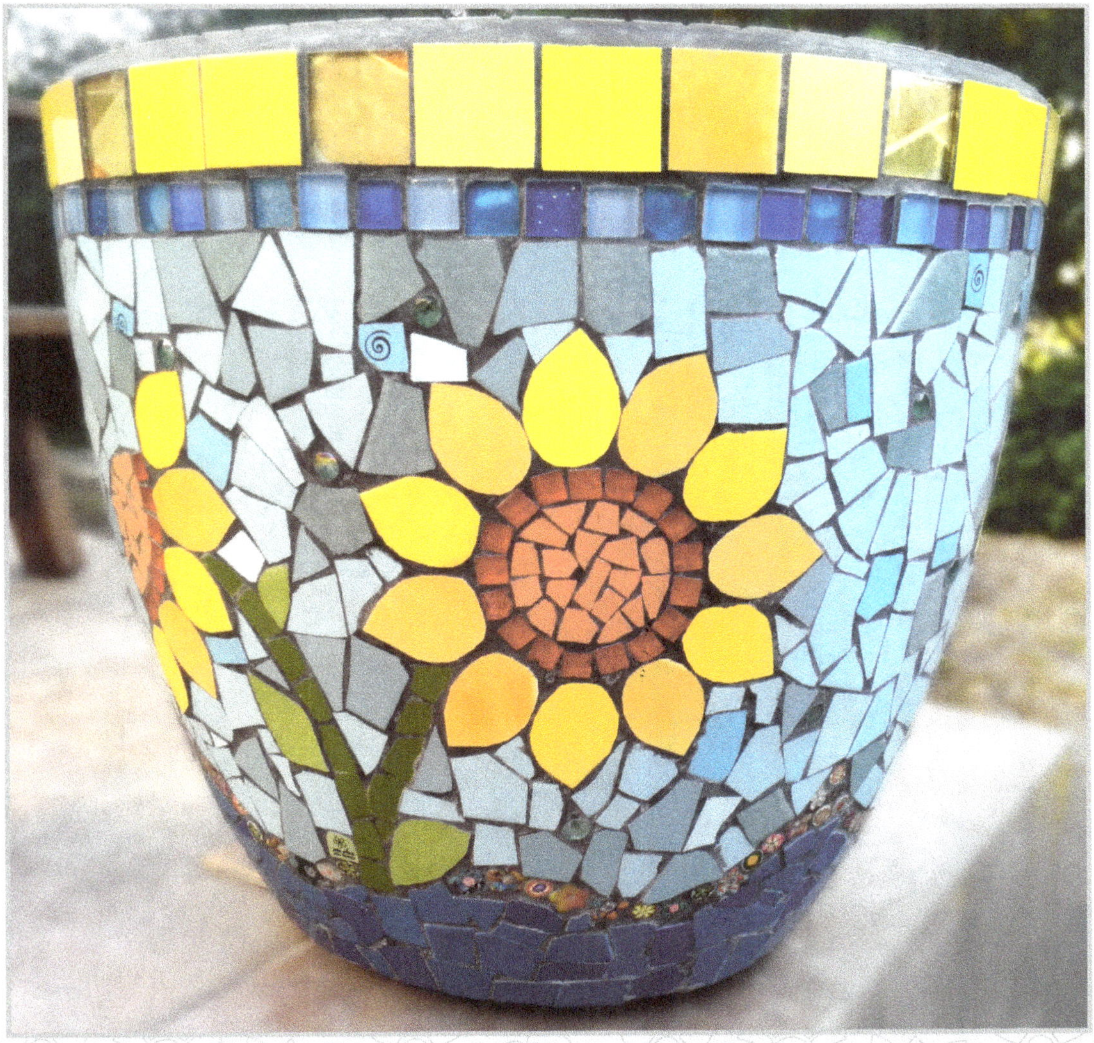

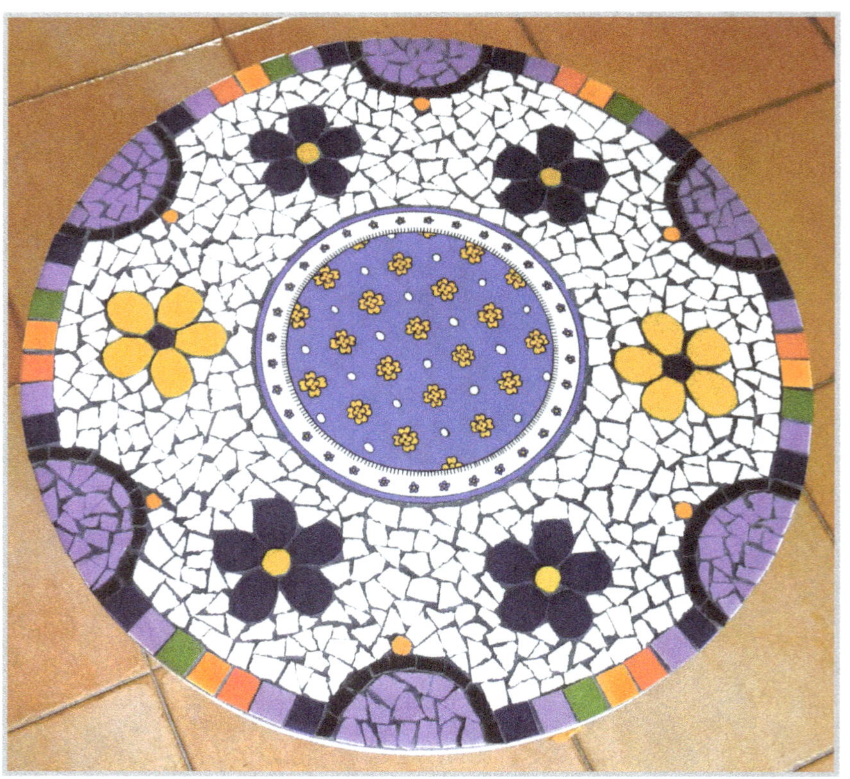

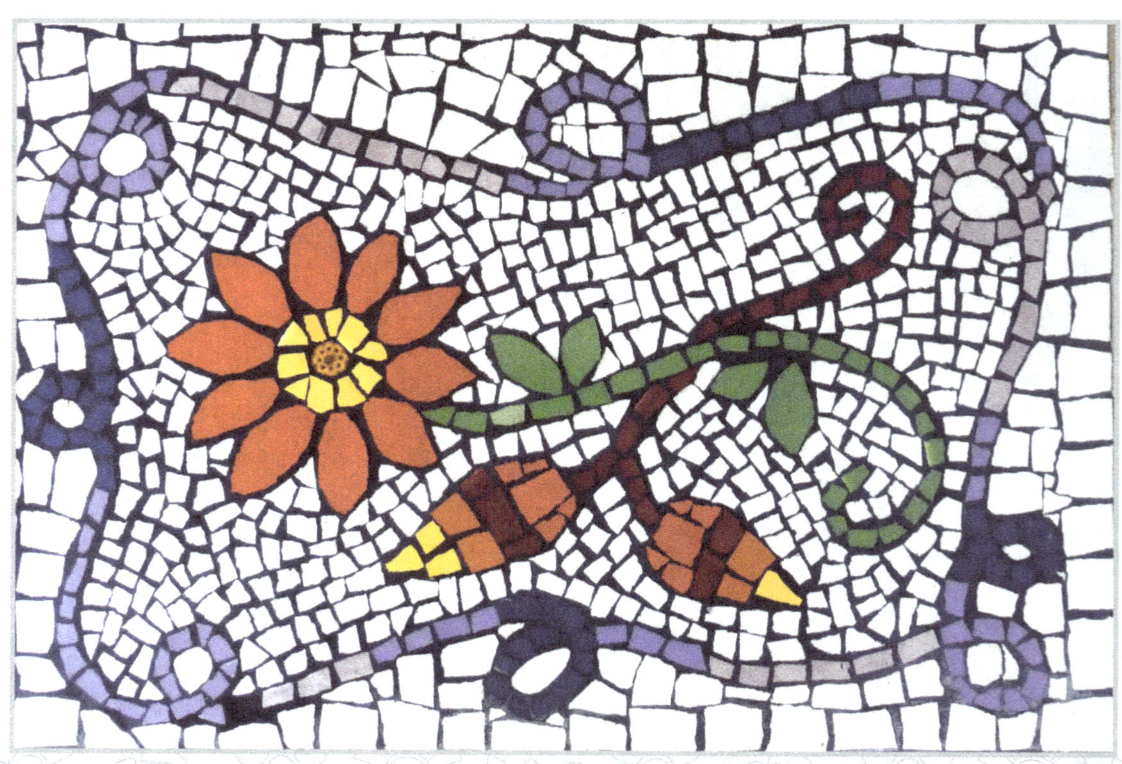

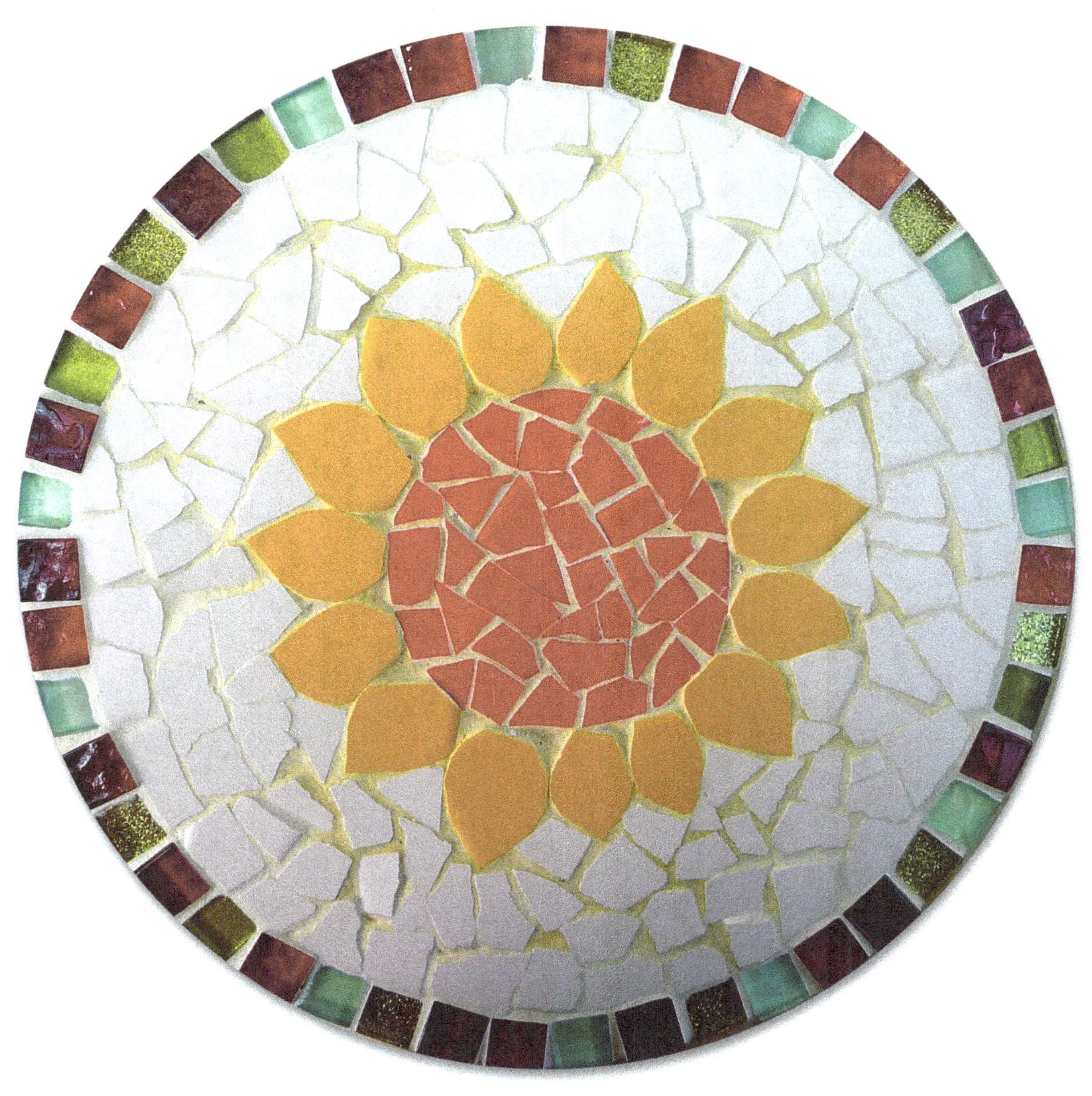

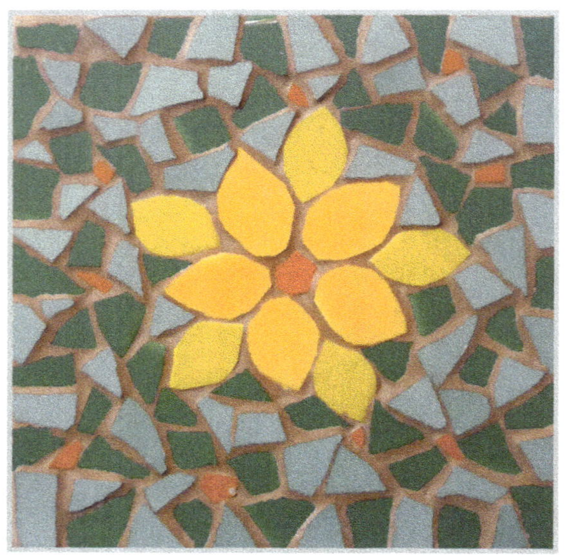

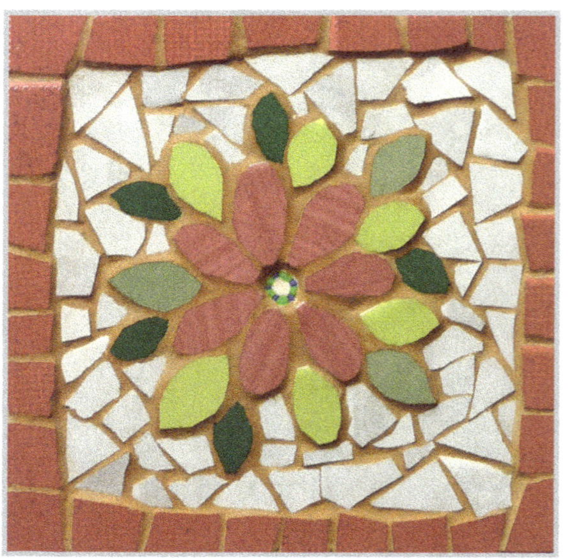

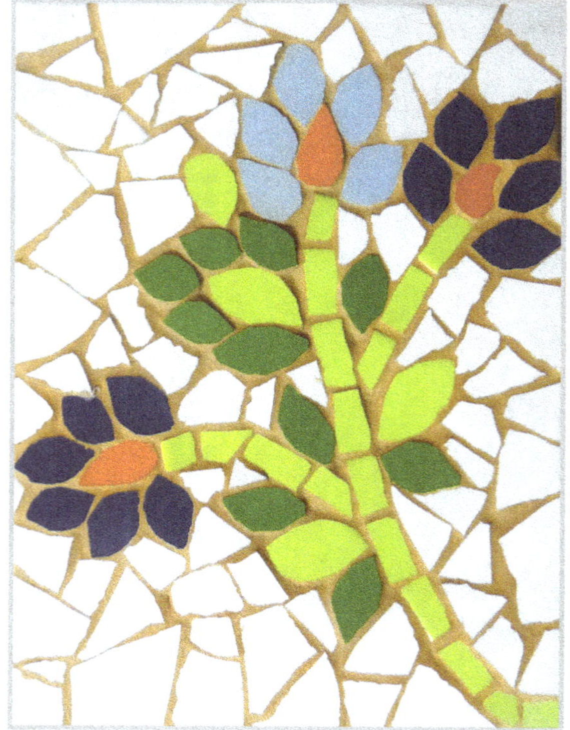

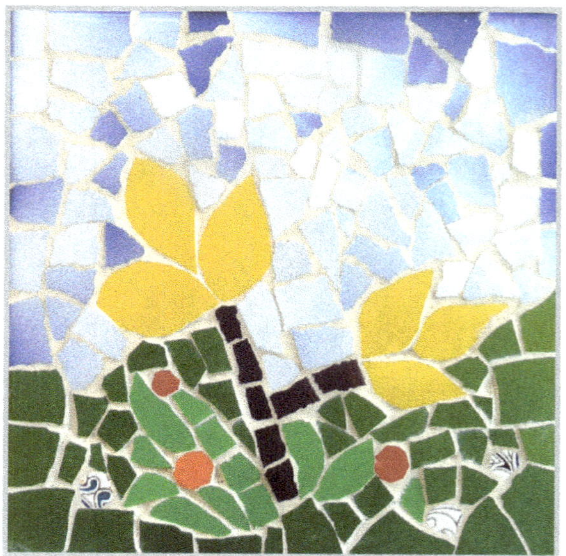

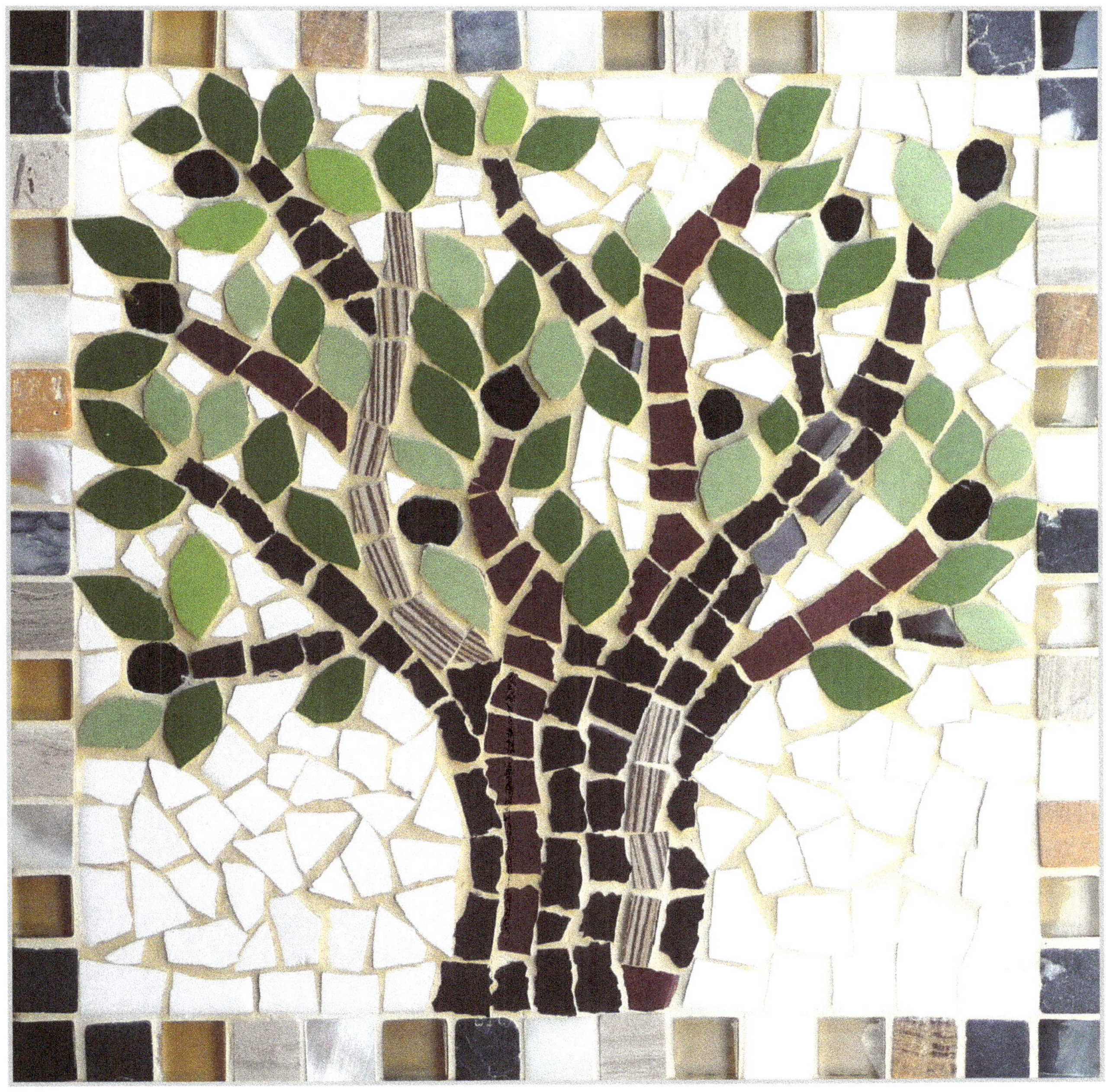

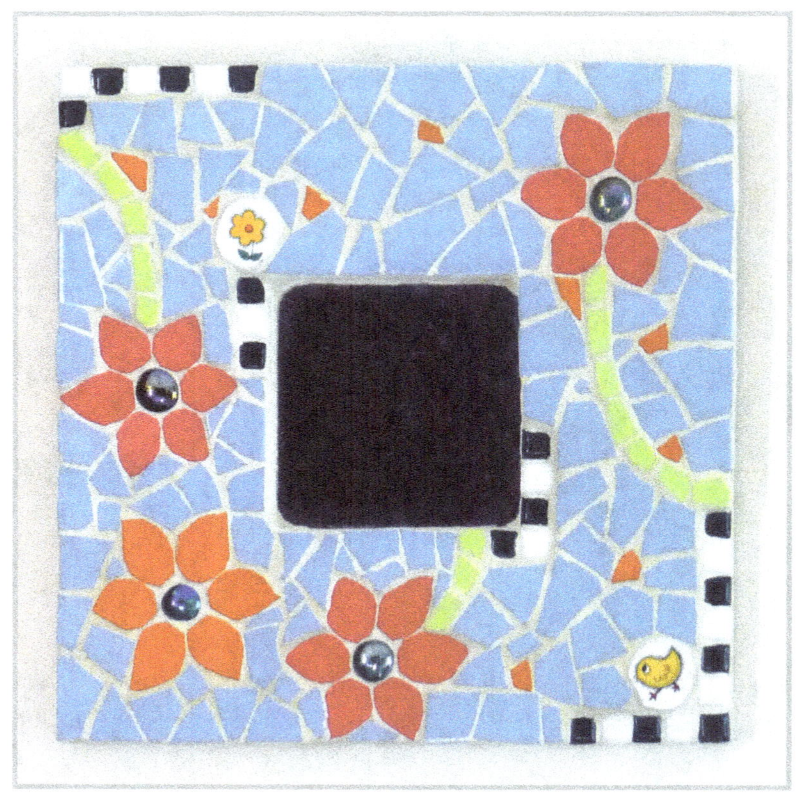

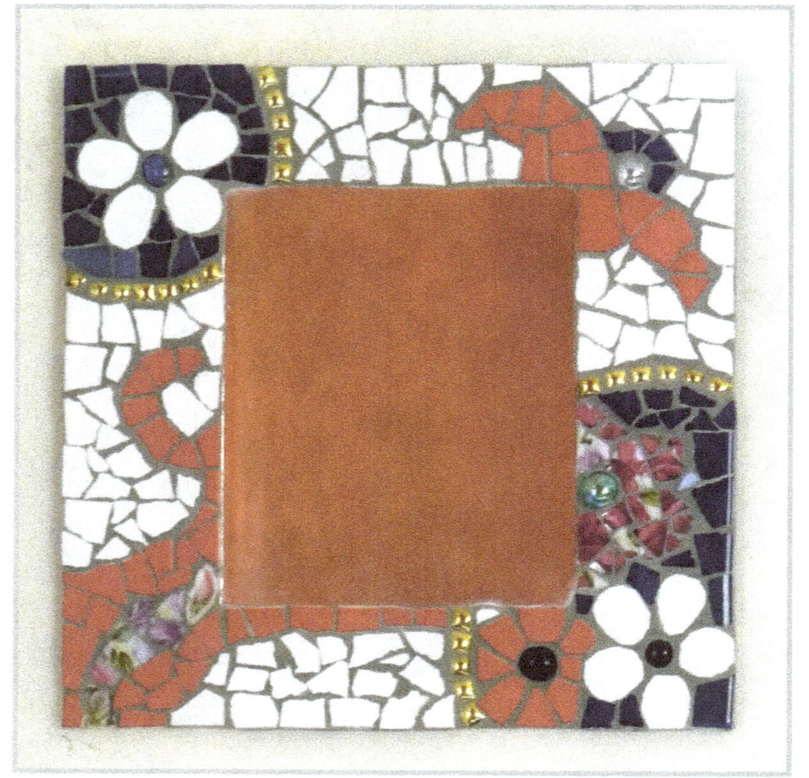

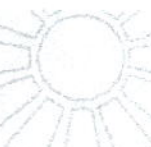

Wheelbarrow

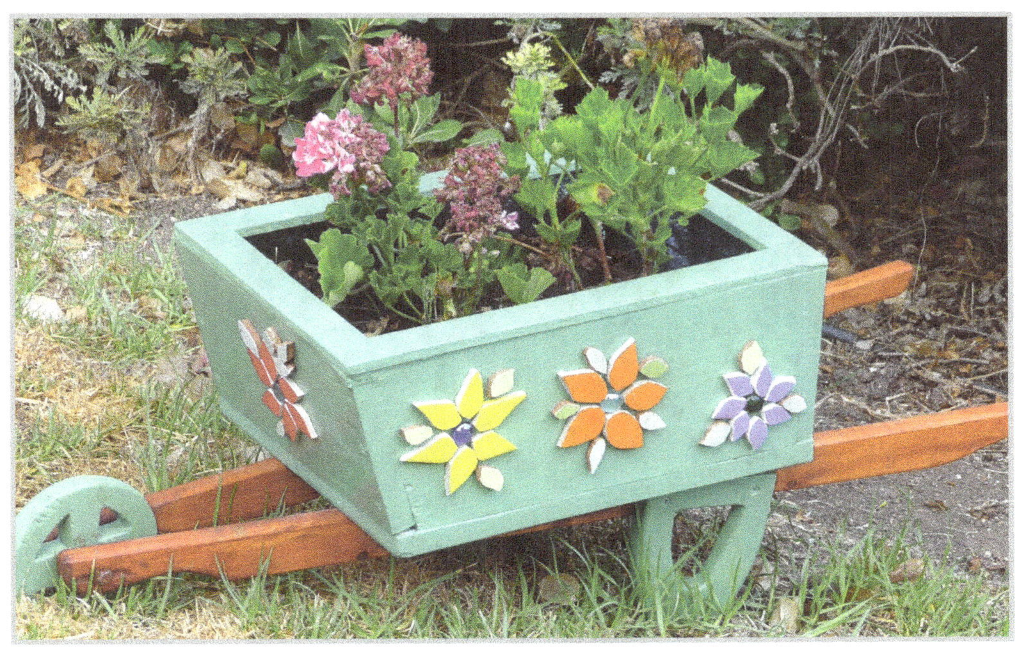

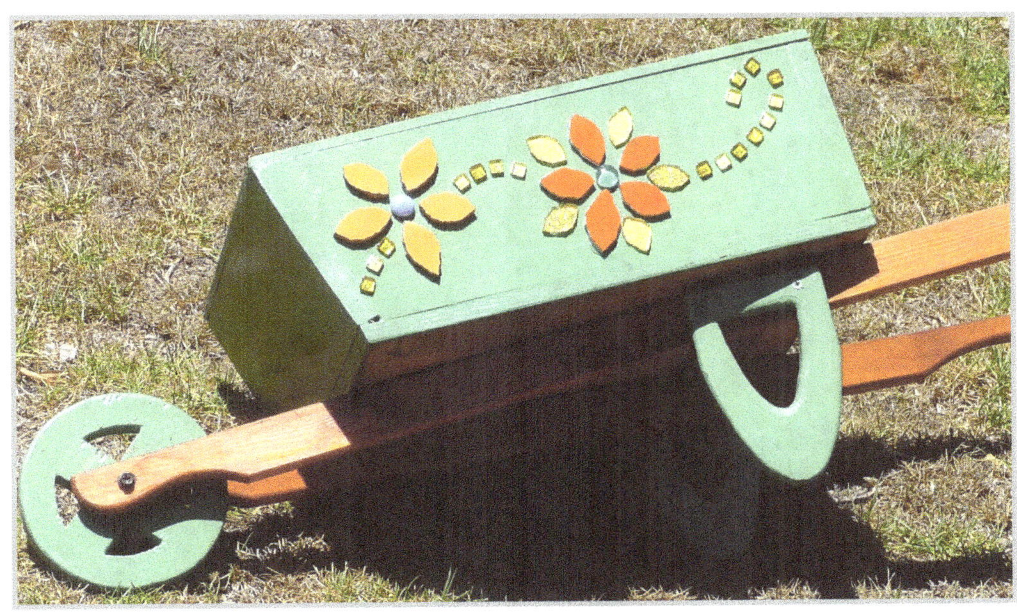

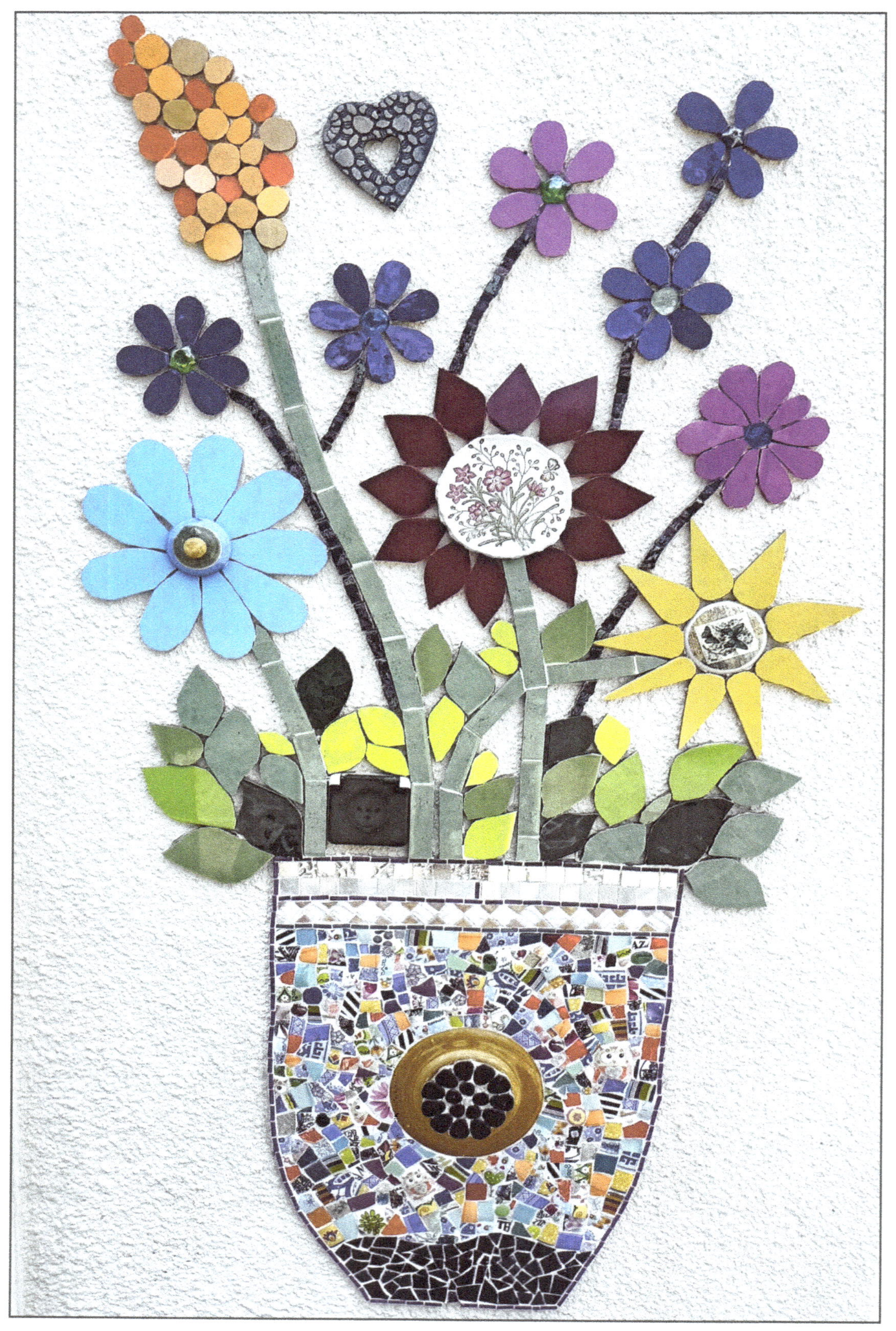

Summary

I hope you have learned something new and thank you for taking the time to read this book.

We have focused on teaching how to cut mosaic flowers. We learned to cut pointed petals, straight petals, and round petals all based on the same cutting technique to create beautiful flowers.

Mosaic flowers do not stand alone, and now you can combine them into any work of art you wish—terracotta pots, mirrors, pictures, signs, and much more! Mosaic flowers will turn any surface into a beautiful and happy one.

Go ahead and apply what we've learned—grab a cutter and some ceramic tiles, choose a base, and start decorating with colorful and beautiful mosaic flowers!

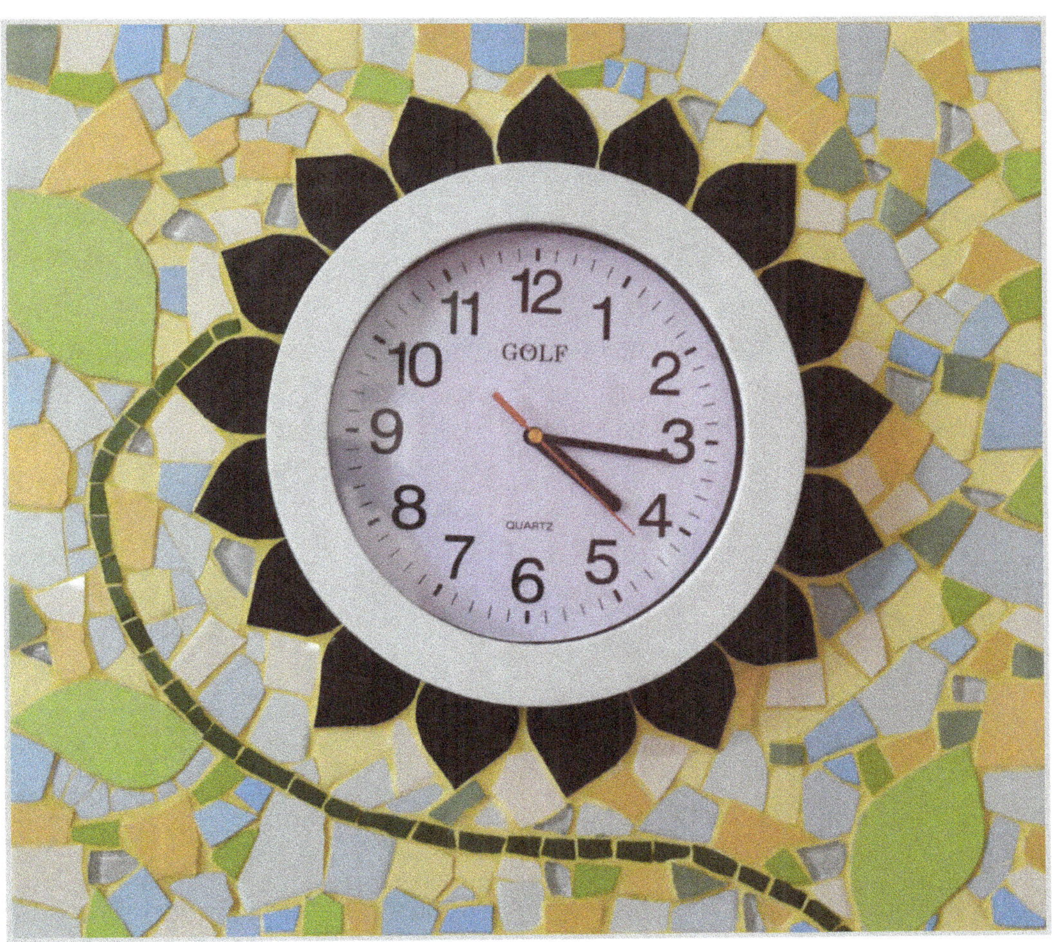

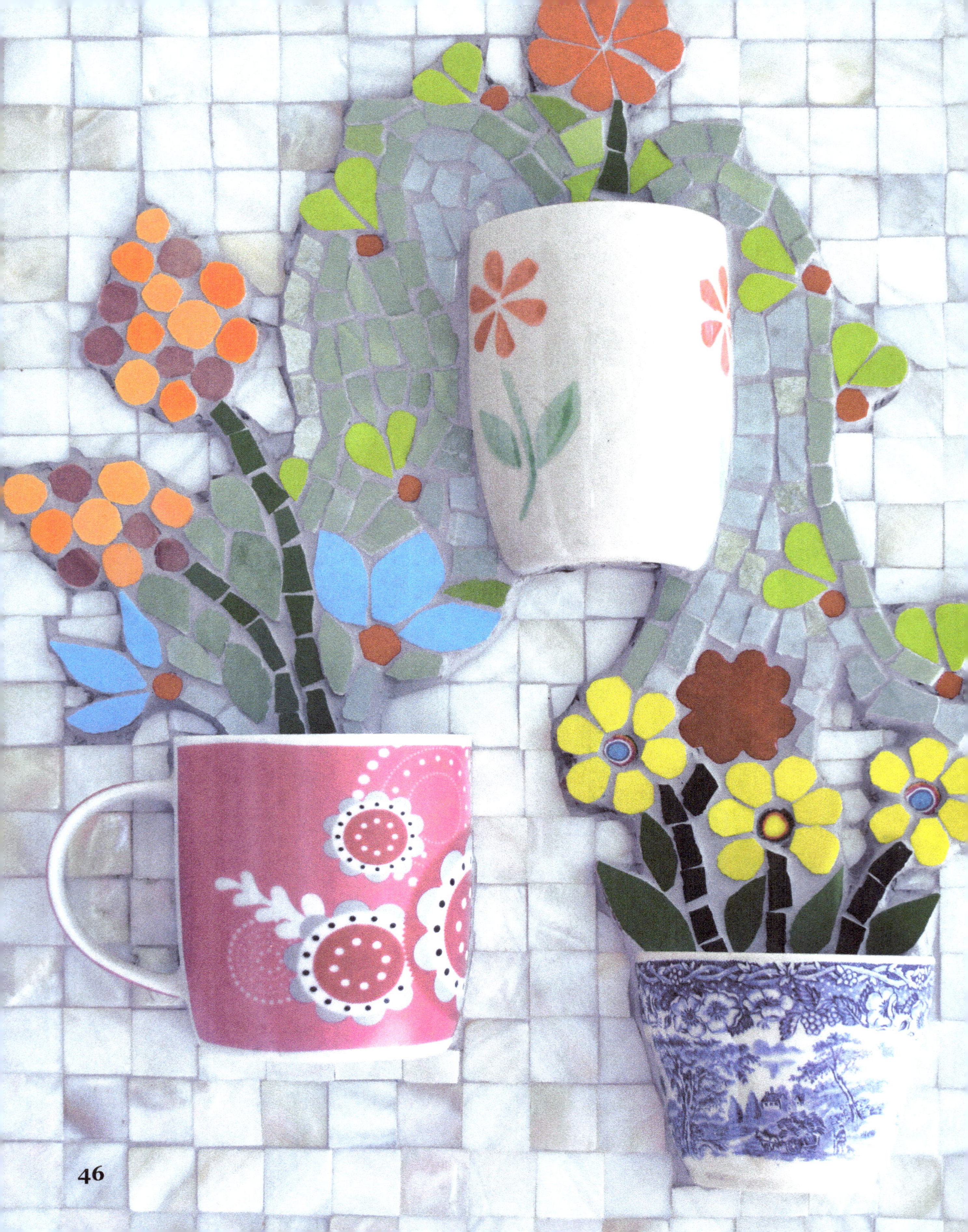

Other books on Amazon:

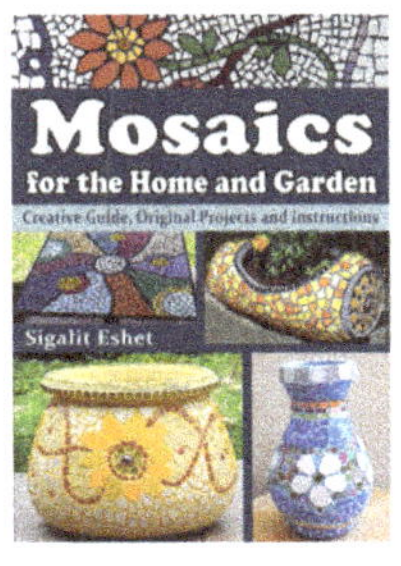 **Mosaics for the Home and Garden**

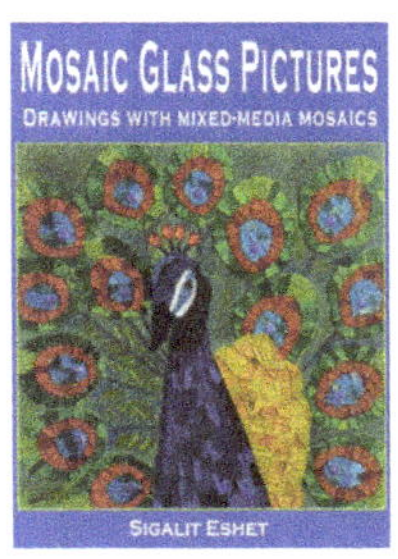 **Mosaic Glass Pictures**

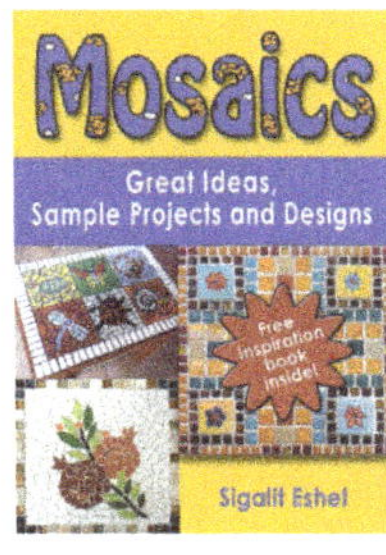 **Mosaics: Great Ideas and Projects**

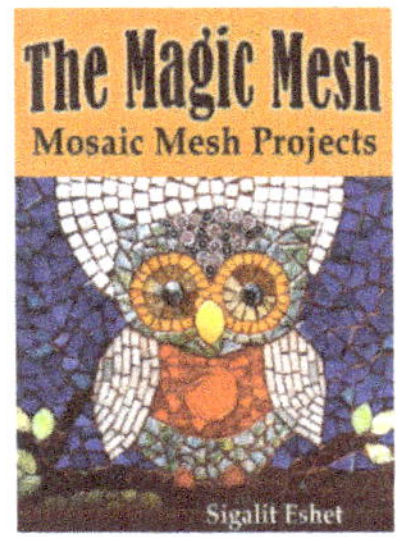 **The Magic Mesh - Mosaic Mesh Projects**

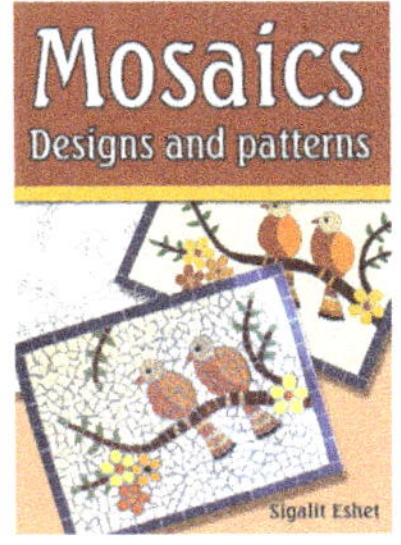 **Mosaics - Designs and patterns**

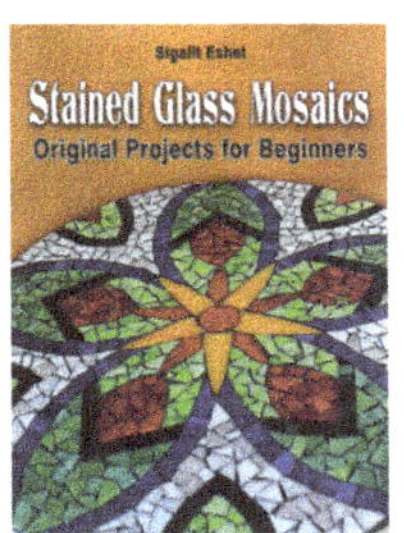 **Stained Glass Mosaic**

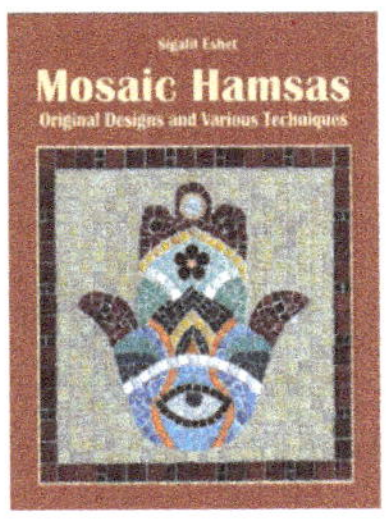 **Mosaic Hamsas**

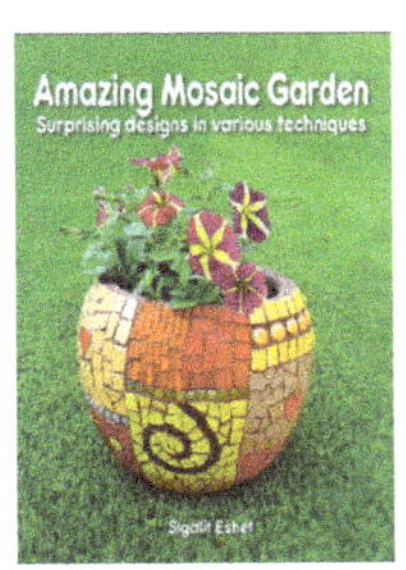 **Amazing Mosaic Garden**

Contact me:

✉ **sigalit@sigalit.art**

🌐 **www.sigalit.art**

f **SigalitBooks**

etsy **Sigalitarts**

a **amazon.com/author/sigaliteshet**

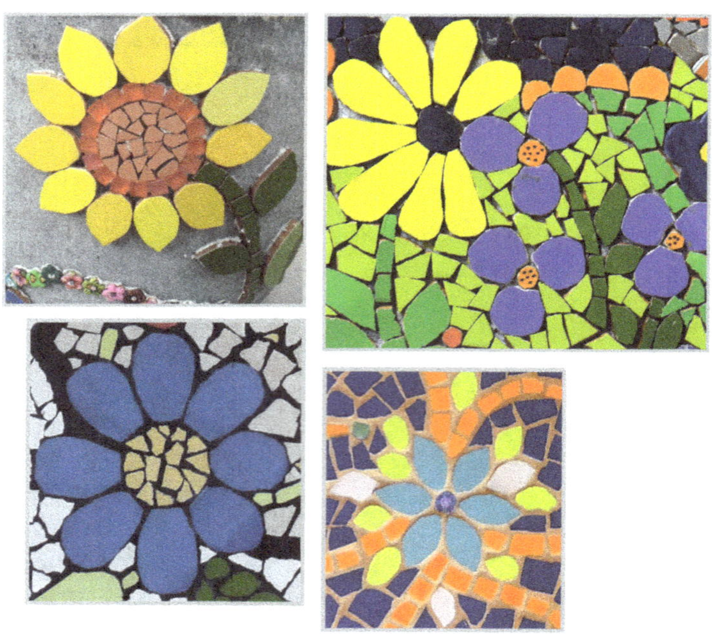